THE **HOPE KNOWS** SERIES:

Getting Through Today

———

Beyond The Past

———

Can God Be Trusted?

———

Facing The Future

HOPE KNOWS

FACING THE
FUTURE

elaine starner

JPV PRESS

For
Caleb, Erin, Marcus,
Brenna, and William

Then the LORD said to me, "Look, Jeremiah!
What do you see?" And I replied, "I see a
branch from an almond tree." And the LORD
said, "That's right, and it means that I am
watching, and I will certainly carry out all
my plans."

– **JEREMIAH 1:11, 12** –

CONTENTS

PRAYER FOR ANXIOUS TIMES:

Listen to my prayer, O God...

for I am overwhelmed by my troubles.

- PSALM 55:1, 2 -

PROMISE OF PEACE

IS IT POSSIBLE?

You will keep in perfect peace all who trust in you, all whose thoughts are fixed on you!

- ISAIAH 26:3 -

"I'll be honest. I'm scared. Really scared," one said.

"The outlook is so gloomy," another added.

"How am I going to make it?" one more wondered.

Anxiety pulsed in the comments around the table. Bodies tensed. Faces strained.

We've all been in similar conversations, haven't we? We look ahead and see nothing hopeful. Worry nags at us, and fear slithers in behind worry. What's going to happen to me?

This particular group was in their mid-sixties, and all seemed healthy. They weren't in danger of imminent physical harm, and judging from their conversation, all had ample financial resources.

But they were having a frank discussion about their fears of getting older and wrangling with medical issues and the health care system. What would the next decade of aging bring? And how would they cope with what was coming?

The same comments could come from a group of twenty-one-year-olds surveying a bleak job market, or forty-five-year-olds watching plummeting stock numbers. These sentiments could be heard from parents sending their twelve-year-old off to junior high, several widows talking over coffee, or employees laid off in a downsizing.

On a larger scale, that conversation could be heard at any time in a country's history—during a time of riots and civil war, under the regime of a persecuting tyrant, as the threatening cloud of nuclear disaster or economic collapse approaches, or—well, just look at the stories on the weather channel these days. Is it any wonder that even the weather has made people nervous and afraid of "what's coming tomorrow"?

We have all stood with our toes on the edge of the future, peering ahead, feeling ripples of anxiety washing into our souls. And sometimes, those ripples swell into raging floods that knock us off our feet and threaten to drown us.

Every now and then, a memory from my childhood comes floating through my day: a small, rectangular plaque hanging on the wall of my Grandma Kate's living room. Do you remember those—painted on glass, often displaying a Bible verse surrounded with flowers, and hung by the same chain that edged the picture? The one in my memory said, in that poetic language of the King James Version, "Thou wilt keep him in perfect peace, whose mind is stayed on thee" (Isaiah 26:3).

It was a lovely, comforting sentiment to my young mind. But as I grew older, it seemed that the script of my life included more and more situations, people, and incidents that shattered any possibility of my life knowing perfect peace.

Yet, there it is, in the Word of God—a promise to us of peace for our anxiety-weary minds and hearts.

As we look at the world around us and hear a battery of grim forewarnings of what could be coming tomorrow, we wonder, *Can peace be possible? And if it is possible, how and where can I find it?*

MORE: Psalm 55:22; Psalm 9:9; Psalm 33:18

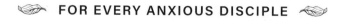 FOR EVERY ANXIOUS DISCIPLE

"Do not let your hearts be troubled and do not be afraid."
[Jesus speaking]
‑ JOHN 14:27 NIV ‑

It would have been enough to send me into a panicked tizzy.

Picture this: As you sit down to dinner with a dear friend, he says: "I have looked forward to having this meal with you before all my suffering begins."

That's what Jesus said to His inner circle one night. What a way to open dinner conversation! As the evening went on, He talked of hard times ahead.

Did they sit in stunned silence? Were their faces grim, their eyes glued to Jesus' face as He talked of hard times coming? Did they feel the creep of fear as He told them they would soon face trouble and harassment because they followed Him? They had already experienced criticism and some open hostility because they were Jesus' followers, but now Jesus said people would hate them, expel them from places of worship, and even try to kill them.

As if all that weren't enough cause for worry, Jesus gave them the explosive news that He knew one of them was a traitor, plotting against Him. And the worst, most shattering development of all: Jesus announced He was going off somewhere— they weren't quite sure where. They would be left behind and on their own, right in the middle of these distressing dangers He had just described.

Imagine the flood of fear that must have washed over them.

Yet embedded within all of those frightening predictions, Jesus talked about peace. "I'm leaving you with a gift—peace of mind and heart. Peace that you will never get from the world. I'm telling you all this so your joy will be complete" (John 14:27; 15:11 AP).

Isn't that incredible? And impossible? All of this danger and distress ahead, and Jesus was talking about peaceful minds and hearts filled with complete joy?

What do you suppose the disciples were thinking? Jesus had given them hope that He would bring about events so that their world and history might take a happier turn. The conversation around the table that night crushed all those hopes they had for the future. I'm sure they wondered, as we do when we ponder our possible future, *If these terrible things are coming, how is an untroubled heart even possible? How can I have peace and joy?*

And they didn't know it then, but they were within hours of events that would be terrifying. Two days later, on a dark, fearful Saturday, they huddled in hiding because Jesus had been executed and they were fearful of what was going to happen to them, as His followers. Do you suppose they remembered then what Jesus had said about trusting Him and having peace of mind and joyful hearts? I can imagine them shaking their heads and saying, "I don't understand. What could He have meant? Look at what's happening! How could He have promised us that?"

Imagine it.

But we don't have to imagine, do we? We know all about such fears and worry and questions.

Let's acknowledge our fears about the future, because Jesus' words and promises that night were also meant for His followers at all times of history. His words are also for you and me, my sisters and brothers, in the time and circumstances of our lives today as we face our own tomorrows.

I don't know where you are now. You could be realizing that your dearest dreams are not going to come true. The stretch of road ahead of you looks rough and treacherous. Life is going to be hard. Perhaps you're facing a serious health issue. Or your spouse has died or moved out. Or you've been put on probation at work because you've talked too much about your faith. Or all those unexpected expenses have eaten up your savings. Or your children are leaving the nest—much too young, you think, to deal with the world, and you aren't happy with the path they've chosen. Or the news broadcasts are headlining yet another terrorist attack and nuclear threats around the world. Or you've looked in the mirror and realized how much your body has aged in the last few years.

Or the wrong president and party came to power in the last election.

Your own experience has confirmed the truth of Jesus' words: No thing, no person, no place in this world can give us peace of mind and heart. Instead, in this earthly life, we have constant cause to fear and fret.

But can we believe that Jesus' words about perfect peace and joy are also true? Can followers of Christ expect peace of mind? Or is it all just a fairy tale, a mirage that won't hold up in the desert heat of change, uncertainty, and fear?

That's what our hope wants to know.

MORE: Psalm 27:14; Psalm 34:15; Micah 7:7

 **WHERE DO WE LOOK FOR HOPE?**

"Trust in God, and trust also in me." [Jesus speaking]
- JOHN 14:1 -

He was a man who had more troubles than most of us. People betrayed him, enemies hunted him, his wife married another man while he was away from home, his son tried to kill him. At times, he wondered where God was and if God knew and cared about what was happening to him.

David, writer of many beloved psalms, knew all this trouble. Yet he had apparently found the secret; his writings overflow with the joy and peace for which we all have a deep longing. Smack dab in the middle of terrifying and devastating trouble, David spoke of peace. Almost every page of the psalms tells us something about joy and peace replacing fear and worry.

At one place, David wrote, "I prayed to the LORD, and he answered me. He freed me from all my fears" (Psalm 34:4).

Can the calming of our fears be that simple? Isn't life in this world much more complicated than that? We might think so. But if we've chosen to believe what God has to say, then let's listen to His words. Let's take them to heart—literally, take them and let them work in our hearts.

If you've never had a discussion with yourself and settled these questions, take some time to do that now:

- Where do I set my sights when I'm looking for hope?
- Where is a safe place to put my trust?
- On whom do I depend to tell me the truth about myself, my circumstances, what is going on in the world, and what is going to happen to the world and to me personally?
- Where do I find security?

David gives us advice on where to look for answers: "O God our savior. You are the hope of everyone on earth" (Psalm 65:5).

Our hope is God our Rescuer. That's the meaning of the word *savior.* David's declaration is clear: Everyone looking for hope must come to this God, the one who rescues. And that's where we are starting as we look for hope for the future. We are looking to God.

Throughout the Scriptures, we find many promises for those who look to God for hope. Here's just a sampling. Which one lights a longing in your heart? Take it and claim it as a promise from God especially for you.

Those who trust the LORD will be joyful. (Proverbs 16:20)

Those who trust in the LORD will find new strength. They will soar high on wings like eagles. They will run and not grow weary. They will walk and not faint. (Isaiah 40:31)

Those who trust in the LORD are as secure as Mount Zion; they will not be defeated but will endure forever. (Psalm 125:1)

"Those who hope in me will not be disappointed." (Isaiah 49:23 NIV, God speaking to His people.)

Those who keep their eyes on the Lord will be delivered from the traps of the enemy. (Psalm 25:15 AP)

Those who trust in Him will be filled with peace, joy, and hope. (Romans 15:13 AP)

"Those who listen to my message and believe in God who sent me have eternal life. They will never be condemned for their sins, but they have already passed from death into life." (John 5:24, Jesus speaking)

Look at that list: joy, strength, peace, no disappointment, security, victory, and living without fear of condemnation. That kind of life may sound like an impossibility in today's world, especially as we look toward the future. But the Creator, the Lord of the Universe, promises that this is what life will be like for those who look to Him for hope.

That's where we want to go in this book— meditating together on God's promises for our lives in the future. What answers and antidotes does God have for the worry and fear that can paralyze us?

Compare the list of promises to the headlines of today. And then remember this: We who put our trust in God can believe in and expect things the rest of the world would call impossibilities.

MORE: Psalm 121:2; Psalm 46:1-3, 10, 11; Psalm 62:5

🌿 YOUR CHOICES 🌿

Trust in the LORD always,
for the LORD God is the eternal Rock.
- ISAIAH 26:4 -

The opening verse immediately follows the "perfect-peace" verse. This line tells us why we must look to the Almighty Creator as our only God.

Humans have a need for a god. No matter who and what we are, we are looking for something more than ourselves. As we look for hope, help, and happiness, we might idolize a person, an ideal, a philosophy, attributes, or achievements. Humanity worships at the altars of—and makes sacrifices to—many gods. Some people look inward for their god, thinking that within themselves they can find the More, the Greater, that is so desired and needed. We've tried many alternatives in our search for peace and security, but we've been disappointed, abandoned, or betrayed.

The Creator God says there is only one place to go for help, hope, and happiness. He alone is the Rock. The strong. The unchangeable. The One who will not disappear. He does not lie to you, and He will keep His promises. He is the only god who will not disappoint you.

One of my favorite promises for those who trust in the Lord is presented in the words of Jeremiah the prophet:

Blessed are those who trust in the LORD and have made the LORD their hope and confidence. They are like trees planted along a riverbank, with roots that reach deep into the water. Such trees are not bothered by the heat or worried by long months of drought. Their leaves stay green, and they never stop producing fruit. (Jeremiah 17:7, 8)

This is the life I want. I want to be a tree planted by the water, with roots that go deep into the source of life, staying strong through tests of heat and drought, always green, continually productive.

The words of the Lord portraying a tree by the water are preceded by another image, one so grim and devastating that I shudder to think of dwelling there.

This is what the LORD says: "Cursed are those who put their trust in mere humans, who rely on human strength and turn their hearts away from the LORD. They are like stunted shrubs in the desert, with no hope for the future. They will live in the barren wilderness, in an uninhabited salty land." (Jeremiah 17:5, 6)

Strong words: *Cursed. No hope for the future. Barren wilderness. Stunted shrubs. Salty land.*

We have all spent some time in that desolate

land. Some of us have dwelt there for years, some for shorter periods of time. We've tasted what life is like in that place—when we have put all our hopes and dreams somewhere other than God, and then the job disappeared or the bank account shriveled. Perhaps the person we thought would love us and support us and have our back forever suddenly turned away, or our health or strength or mind was no longer dependable, or the ideology we believed in turned sour. We know what that salty, parched land looks like. We know how it feels, and we know how hope withers and dies in that wilderness.

What a contrast to the tree that is always green and bearing fruit because it's deeply connected to the source of life!

God put those two images right next to each other to make His point: We have to make a choice. Where will we look for hope? Where will we put our trust? Who or what will we revere and worship?

Our Creator, the one who made our hearts and understands everything about us, says there is only one place to find the hope that brings peace and joy: We'll find it through trust in Him because He is the eternal Rock.

You will need to choose. In which place do you want to live?

But even before that decision must come another: Will we believe what God has told us?

We make many choices every day, choices about who and what we trust. Every time our choice is to believe and trust God, we send our roots deeper and deeper into the life-giving water, the source of peace.

Will we believe what He says? That's the key question.

If there is peace and joy to be found as I face tomorrow and next week and next year, then I want it. I'm determined not to be a stunted shrub in the barren desert, with no hope for the future. I want to be a tree by the water.

My choice is to believe God. If that's the choice you've made, too, then let's listen together and hear what He has to tell us about the future—and our hope.

MORE: Psalm 118:8; Psalm 146:3-10; Isaiah 44:8

 **GUARDED**

The LORD gives His people strength.
The LORD blesses His people with peace.
- **PSALM 29:11** -

I ended that last meditation with the words, "I'm determined." I am. I've decided I'm going to be a tree by the water. I want a life of fearlessness and fruitfulness. I'm going to believe and trust God.

That's so easy to type this morning, on a beautiful summer day, after a good night's rest and an hour or so of contemplating these Scriptures.

But what about those mornings when I haven't slept much because my mind could not let go of some worry? When I'm faced with a week that scares me? When I'm troubled by a relationship conflict that seems unresolvable? When I am nagged by doubts brought on by a scathing criticism? When I don't know how I'm going to pay all the bills this month? When—

You can add many of your own situations. And in many of those circumstances, our determination falters. Our trust wavers. Our faith stumbles. We are afraid.

What then? Are we doomed to be stunted shrubs in the barren wilderness with no hope for the future?

No!

Jesus the Rescuer is always with us. Always.

He's come to live with everyone who believes in Him. If we've opened the door when He knocked, He's living right here with us. And although we might falter, waver, or stumble, He does not.

A few pages back, we looked at the wonderful promises God makes to those who seek Him. Those promises don't depend on our determination or our willpower. We too easily falter and waver. That's one of the reasons we need a Rescuer.

Look more closely at the perfect-peace verse (Isaiah 26:3). It's not that we will *stay* in perfect peace. No, we are *kept* in perfect peace.

The letter to believers in Philippi has good advice for us when we are faltering:

> Don't worry about anything; instead, pray about everything. Tell God what you need, and thank him for all he has done. Then you will experience God's peace, which exceeds anything we can understand. His peace will guard your hearts and minds as you live in Christ Jesus. (Philippians 4:6, 7)

When we feel worry sneaking in, we need concrete actions to take, and here they are:

- Pray about everything.
- Tell God what we need.
- Remember everything He's already done and thank Him.

Pray. Tell. Thank.

Simple steps to follow when we feel worry shoving its way into our heads and hearts.

The next lines tell us the results of Pray/Tell/Thank—we will experience God's peace.

Did you notice the two sentences describing this peace of God?

First, it's miraculous. That means it won't be logical or explainable. It will be so amazing, even you can't understand how it's come about. You want a miracle? Here is one—His peace replacing your worry. It's one of God's promises to His children.

Second, it is not something we find and grab and hold onto ourselves. Instead, God's peace is the active agent, and we are the recipient. Our hearts and minds are *guarded* by the peace God gives. I like to visualize the peace of God—whatever it may look like—standing guard all around the perimeter of my heart and mind, protecting, defending, and shielding from those attacks of fear and worry.

This miraculous peace doesn't depend on us, our feelings, or our determination and strength. It depends on the God who cares about us, who knows what we need before we even ask, and who has a vast store of goodness to pour into our lives. This God holds us—even when we're unable to hold onto Him.

Pray. Tell. Thank. And then, even when we're faltering, we'll be guarded and held and *kept*.

I trust the God who has promised that.

MORE: Deuteronomy 33:27; Psalm 5:11, 12; 2 Thessalonians 3:16

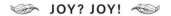 JOY? JOY!

And the hillsides blossom with joy.
- **PSALM 65:12** -

Have you noticed another word that seems to be tagging along with *peace?* If I counted accurately, the word *joy* has already occurred twelve times in these first pages.

And perhaps you noticed that word persistently popping up because joy seems elusive for you. You've been chasing it, but just as a perfect peace seems impossible, your life knows scant moments of joy. If that's the case, don't close this book and put it away. Keep reading. Let's stay on this journey together. Don't we long for these things? Remember: God has made us promises about peace and joy.

I know I took the opening Scripture out of context, but it presented an image so appealing to me that I've latched onto it and can't let it go. *The hillsides blossoming with joy.* As I stand here, a tree by the water, I also long for joy to burst into bloom on the surrounding hillsides.

We have trouble understanding this word because in our Western culture, *joy*—like *peace*—has taken on a meaning that is dependent on external circumstances. If everything is running smoothly, if things are going our way, if our lives somehow measure up to images we see and messages we hear in the world's media, if everything looks bright and beautiful, *then* we can be joyful.

But take a look at some of the places *joy* appears in the Scriptures. It seems to me that in God's Word, joy is mentioned just as often as peace—and in some of the most unexpected situations.

In the psalms, David gives vent to grief, frustration, or pain too many times to count, yet just as many times he makes a declaration like this, "You have turned my mourning into joyful dancing. You have taken away my clothes of mourning and clothed me with joy" (Psalm 30:11). Does that raise a longing in your soul? Are you ready to shed your clothes of mourning and break into joyful dancing?

In Jesus' words in Luke 6:22,23, He tells us to dance for joy when people hate us, mock us, and even call us evil because we follow Him.

Paul took several paragraphs to list all the trouble he'd been through—beaten, thrown in jail, working to exhaustion, sometimes hungry, scorned and disbelieved, threatened by mobs—and yet he wrote, "Our hearts ache, but we always have joy" (2 Corinthians 6:4-10).

The writer of Hebrews recounts the difficult times of persecution many Christians had been through, including "You... joyfully accepted the confiscation of your property" (Hebrews 10:34 NIV). Where's the joy in those circumstances?

Another apostle wrote that when trouble comes our way, it's an opportunity for joy (James 1:2).

How is all of this possible? Paul wrote, "Whatever happens, my dear brothers and sisters, rejoice in the Lord" (Philippians 3:1). Jesus did talk of an overflowing joy and fullness of joy for His followers, but how is that possible in the face of trouble, threats, and sorrow?

Yet there they are—the promises in God's Word to us: Those who trust in Him will be joyful. Hillsides will blossom with joy. Jesus will fill us with His overflowing joy. We can rejoice in everything that happens.

This joy that God has promised—in all circumstances—must be something far more significant than superficial good feelings that do not last. This joy doesn't depend on the circumstances around us. This joy, like God's peace, must be something miraculous. It must be something that reaches down deep, searching out and satisfying our greatest longings.

Just as in finding a perfect peace, I have a lot to learn about joy—what it is and how I can find it. I'm beginning to get glimpses. My desire is to have more than glimpses; my desire is to have all that God will give me. If fretting and fear can be exchanged for a peace that stands guard over my heart and mind, and if joy can somehow burst into blossom in my world, then that's what I want.

Are you in a similar place? Perhaps you don't quite understand what God means when He's talking about peace and joy, and you certainly don't see how either is possible in today's world and in the face of grim forecasts of the future. But if God really will give us these things, then you and I both want to know and have more.

I do know this for a certainty—we cannot create joy or peace on our own. The world cannot give them to us, at least, not joy and peace of the quality that Jesus promises. Both of these are gifts of our heavenly Father's kindness to His children, and we will see, as we go through these meditations, how miraculously they come to our lives.

So I am pausing at my keyboard now and asking the Spirit to open our eyes as we go forward together on the journey through this book, and to grant us these longed-for gifts. Please, take a minute to do the same. Ask Him for more and more peace and joy. Miraculous peace to guard your heart. Deep joy to water your soul. He hears these prayers.

MORE: Psalm 33:21; Psalm 92:4; Psalm 105:3

✨ MORE AND MORE! ✨

May God give you more and more grace and peace
as you grow in your knowledge of God and Jesus our Lord.

– **2 PETER 1:2** –

Nearly every one of the early Christian letters included in the New Testament opens with greetings from the writer. Most of them include something like, "May God give you grace and peace."

But Peter's greeting differs from all the others in one way—he added another phrase to the usual greeting: "...as you grow in your knowledge of God and Jesus our Lord."

Peter's letter is the only one that adds that second phrase. As we reflect on what we are told of Peter's life, those words ring with the conviction and confidence of personal experience.

The Peter we see in the Gospels struggled in his belief and faith. He was often anxious and worried and floundering. He even turned his back on his dear friend Jesus at the most desperate time. But by the time Peter wrote this letter, he had learned that peace comes when you get to know God and Jesus, and grace and peace flow ever stronger as you grow your relationship with God—in the same way you have, year after year, built your most intimate and enduring human relationships.

Besides that longed-for grace and peace, we

find that we can expect even more as we get to
know our God:

- Knowing God leads to trusting Him because
  we learn His character. (Psalm 9:10)

- Knowing God will help us stand strong
  during coming hard times. (Daniel 11:32)

- Knowing Jesus Christ powers effective and
  productive lives. (2 Peter 1:3, 8)

- Those who "taste and see that the Lord is
  good" will find joy. (There's that promise of
  joy again.) (Psalm 34:8)

From the words of Jesus Himself, as He poured
out His heart to His Father in prayer, we hear that
knowing God and Jesus "is the way to have eternal
life" (John 17:3). When you read the words *eternal
life*, don't limit your thinking to *an immortal life*.
It's true, an eternal life is a life that goes on forever.
But it is also a life lived in heavenly dimensions, a
life that Jesus can give us even while we are still on
this earth.

Christ, our Rescuer, has brought us out of the
kingdom ruled by darkness and given us a life in His
kingdom of light. This is eternal life, and we want
to live here! We want to exchange the gloom that
settles on our hearts, minds, and souls for the light

that no darkness can extinguish. In this kingdom, we can replace fretting with calmness and serenity. Here, hearts and minds are transformed, and lives become vibrant, fruitful, and full of hope—even as we stand and face all the unknowns of tomorrow.

The way to have this life? Get to know God and the one He sent to earth.

God can be known. He wants to be known, even more than He wants our rituals of religion. God promises that He is the same God today as He was in the past and will be in the future and that those who seek Him will find Him. He doesn't dance around, changing with the times or circumstances or popular opinion of Him. He is constant and dependable. And, in His kindness, He came to earth as a man who can guide us to the path to peace (Luke 1:79).

Again and again in Scripture, the great Creator is referred to as the "God of peace." May He give you more and more grace and peace and joy as you learn to know Him better.

MORE: Numbers 6:24-26; John 15:11; John 17:13

PRAYER FROM YOUR PLACE OF PRIVILEGE:

Teach me to do your will. May your Spirit

lead me forward on firm footing.

– PSALM 143:10 AP –

IN A PLACE
OF PRIVILEGE

 WHERE WE NOW STAND

Because of our faith, Christ has brought us into this place
of undeserved privilege where we now stand, and we
confidently and joyfully look forward to sharing God's glory.

- **ROMANS 5:2** -

How did we ever navigate life before GPS was available to us all? I'm continually impressed with the technology that declares I am now crossing Oak Street, and sure enough, I see the street sign telling me I'm crossing Oak Street.

My GPS has been a tremendous help when I need to find my way in an unfamiliar town. But I do miss some of our old ways of doing things. You know, like reading a map, or scratching directions on any handy scrap of paper as someone in the know shares tips on how to get there quickly. Or, even, stopping a friendly-looking person to inquire if *they* know how to get to my destination. The generation who grows up relying only on a GPS will never know such joys.

I used to say that as long as I had a map, I wasn't afraid of taking on the challenge of going anywhere. One year I drove alone into the heart of Chicago, guided only by a map. (I know, I can hardly believe that myself as I look back on that day.)

At a writing workshop close to my home, I met two ladies who had driven over five hundred miles to attend. In the course of our conversation, they asked where they were, exactly. I didn't understand their question. How could they have driven through four states and now be sitting right there with me and still not know where they were?

"Oh," one explained. "We just followed our GPS directions. But we have no idea where we are!"

I do think they knew they were in Ohio, but they had no idea where in Ohio.

A map still has advantages that I am not ready to relinquish. For one thing, it gives me the big picture. I can see the entire route from my starting point to my destination. I can follow my progress along that route and see what is still to come. I enjoy the expectation of what's ahead. I love to watch towns go by. It's good to know where I am in the journey. At those few times when I rely totally on my GPS, I feel disconnected, with no sense of how I arrived or where I am in relation to other cities and geographical points.

This book is about our journey into the future, whether the future is tomorrow or ten years from now or eternity. It's important that we see the big picture and know what is behind us, where we are now, and where we are headed.

Why is knowing all this important?

Because I want you to take joy (yes, joy!) in where you are now. No matter what's going on in the circumstances around you, no matter what grim news makes the headlines today, no matter what storms are brewing within you, I want you to find the joy of where you are.

Read the opening verse again and take it personally. Be sure to note *where* Christ brings us if we put our lives in His hands and have faith in Him.

I'm standing in a place of undeserved privilege? Yes, and so are you, if you have declared your faith in Christ.

Even though we still live earthly lives here in this world, Christ gathers up those who will believe in and trust Him and puts them in a new place. A place of privilege. A place of confidence and joy.

Doesn't that intrigue you?

We did nothing to deserve it. Pause for a moment, and acknowledge that.

Our feet have been placed here. They have not found this place on their own. They haven't worked hard to get here. They have not earned this privileged spot.

Jesus Christ has put us here. He is the Rescuer.

Where is this place? We might better ask, *what* is this place where we now stand?

I wanted to know. And I found that the answer reveals one of those treasures that the more you dig, the more you find and the more excited you get, and so you dig all the more, and you find all the more, and you are delighted more and more.

What I found was so important to my life that I want to share it with you.

MORE: Psalm 103:1-5; Ephesians 3:6; Colossians 1:12, 13

 **GOD OF RESTORATION**

He heals the brokenhearted and bandages their wounds.

– **PSALM 147:3** –

I will never forget one scene from my teenage years. At a youth retreat, talking to a small group of us teenagers, our pastor cupped his hands as though he were protecting a single, delicate stalk of grass or sheltering a flickering flame about to expire. We could see the images as we heard his quiet, confident words: "He promised that a bruised reed He will not break, and a smoldering wick He will not extinguish."

My memory holds nothing else about that day. I can't tell you who else was in the group, the subject of the Bible study, or even where it all happened. But the Spirit has kept the image of protecting hands and the comforting, tender words in my mind.

I've been a bruised reed, wounded, fragile, likely to break apart completely if one more blow comes against it. Or a smoldering wick, its power and potential almost snuffed out. Are you either of those? Or have you been there?

Our pastor was quoting a prophecy of Isaiah. Matthew, the disciple of Jesus, recalled those words as he watched Jesus' tenderness in healing the sick and restoring broken bodies and spirits. Jesus fulfilled that prophecy during His time on earth—and He's continuing that healing during our day, too. He is the same tender, healing Rescuer that He was two thousand years ago.

In this place of privilege, the power of the past is broken.

I don't know what blows and slashes have come against your body and spirit, or how your life has been torn. Every morning, physical or emotional pain may make it difficult for you to get out of bed. Your days may be shrouded and blurred with grief or hobbled by pain or throbbing with anger. Perhaps hard times in your pilgrimage have left you exhausted and frail. You are ready to break. Your energy and potential are almost snuffed out.

What my hope does know is that the Kingdom of God is here and now, and the King is alive and working in His kingdom, healing and restoring. Ever since Adam and Eve lost their paradise existence in Eden, God has planned to restore life to those who come to Him. I believe that with all my heart and soul. I've seen it. Whether it's miraculous physical healing or healing of mind and heart that is needed, God can heal the rips and tears and diseases the past has thrust into our lives. It's happening right now, in this world, and complete restoration will come in the next age.

Throughout the Gospels, we read about the crowds of sick people coming to the man they had heard could heal diseases and infirmities. They were desperate, and they came in the hope that Jesus would help them. My maladies and wounds were not physical; they were emotional, mental, and spiritual, but I was just as desperate as those crowds besieging Jesus. I kept going back to the promises of healing and restoration I found in God's words to us. One of my favorites is found in Ezekiel (yes, that "strange" book).

This is a prophecy given to the Israelites who were living in exile. Their peaceful existence—indeed, their entire lives—had been smashed by a foreign power. Their land had been torn apart by war, cities destroyed, fields stripped and left barren, and many of the people taken to a foreign country as prisoners of war. That was the past that had broken them, left them devastated. Then they received God's promises through Ezekiel.

That's also a fairly accurate description of my emotional and relational landscape at the bleakest time of my life, a time when I often searched out God's promises to heal and restore, a time when I began to see what those promises mean to us who are hurting.

God's message of hope coming through Ezekiel was that He was going to bring the exiles back to their own country. The nation would be restored. Cities would be rebuilt, and the land that had been laid waste would be productive again. The wilderness would burst into bloom, and withered trees would once again flourish and produce.

Let these words sink into your soul because His promises of healing and restoration are also for us today. History has put us in different times, but God's character and care for His children do not change. His promise stands:

And when I bring you back, people will
say, This former wasteland is now like the
Garden of Eden!... Then the surrounding
nations that survive will know that I, the
LORD, have rebuilt the ruins and replanted
the wasteland. For I, the LORD, have spoken,
and I will do what I say. (Ezekiel 36:35, 36)

Notice how firmly He says, "I've said I will do it,
and I will!"

How I longed for my ruins to be rebuilt and my
wastelands to be like the Garden of Eden. Perhaps
that's why, way back in my teen years, the Spirit
of God sealed that promise in my heart and mind—
so that I would always remember that the Rescuer
would not break this bruised reed or extinguish the
smoldering wick.

And I tell you now—only the Lord could rebuild
my life. There was no other hope. He is the one who
replanted and transformed. He is still in the process
of planting, pulling out weeds, and pruning. The
wasteland is gone, and He is still creating in the
garden.

As I stand in this place of privilege and look
backward at my journey, my hope knows this about
the past: The kingdom of God is here, now, and my
God rebuilds, restores, and replants.

He waits for us to come to Him. And when we

do, He hears with love and heals with compassion. He's said He will do it.

MORE: Psalm 30:2; Psalm 107:19, 20; Isaiah 30:18, 19; Isaiah 53:5

CANCELED!

He canceled the record of the charges against us
and took it away by nailing it to the cross.
‑ **COLOSSIANS 2:14** ‑

But...

Are you thinking the same thing I have thought?

But what if the shackles of the past are of our own making? What if we are like those prisoners described in Psalm 107 who sit "in darkness and deepest gloom, imprisoned in chains of deepest misery" because they rebelled against the words of God, scorning the counsel of the Most High? What if that is our past?

We all have a past. Our past is, simply, what has transpired previously. And all of us, whether nineteen or ninety, have years of living behind us. A history.

These days, though, the words *past* and *history* imply much more than just events over a passage of time. The words imply a *record*. When we have "a past" or "a history," a list of wrongdoings, unwise choices, or destructive and shameful behavior follows us throughout our days.

This may be our prison—our shame and guilt over what we have done. Jesus can set us free from those chains, too. The hope for our past is this: For anyone who belongs to Christ, that record is canceled! The list was nailed to the cross where Jesus died, and God has forgiven us.

I know that I will someday stand before the judgment throne, and I will deserve a sentence of punishment for who and what I've been. But there will be no record against me. It's been canceled.

I cannot describe to you the feelings that come over me when I think of that time. My hope knows that all record of the sins of my past has been destroyed. Wiped clean. Canceled. Gone. Forgotten. Forever. It's difficult for our human minds to comprehend such a thing. Our world doesn't work like that. But that's what God's Word promises. Jesus took care of that for me, and it's part of the reality of our place of privilege.

Then, when Jesus was resurrected from the dead to a new life, He also gave us hope of a new life. The old is dead, and its power is broken. The new has come. It's not just a "second chance." It's an entirely new life on a new level with a new relationship to God and a long, long list of new realities in which we are privileged to live.

My past life truly was "another lifetime" because God birthed a new life in me. And, according to His plan for everybody who believes, He took me in and adopted me as His child—instead of condemning me.

No, I didn't do a thing to deserve this new life as a daughter of the King of the Universe. Jesus came to my rescue, and He is the one who brought me to this place of undeserved privilege.

MORE: Psalm 107:10-15; Romans 8:1; 1 Peter 2:24

✧ INHERITANCE ✧

[The Father] has enabled you to share in the inheritance that belongs to his people, who live in the light. For he has rescued us from the kingdom of darkness and transferred us into the Kingdom of his dear Son, who purchased our freedom and forgave our sins.

- COLOSSIANS 1:12-14 -

Cinderella.

That name alone calls forth certain thoughts and images, doesn't it? A poor girl living as a degraded servant finds her life taking an amazing turn, and she becomes a princess!

It's the stuff of fairy tales: paupers who become rich, frogs turning to royalty, beasts that regain their humanity. We've even coined a phrase, using the words "a Cinderella story" to describe sports teams, business ventures, or rags-to-riches life accounts.

The description in Colossians 1 (quoted at the opening of this meditation) is not a fairy tale. This is what God says about the place we now stand, this place of undeserved privilege: God moved us from slavery in a dark kingdom to freedom in His own Kingdom. He forgave our sins, though we could never earn or deserve that, or repay Him. And look at that opening line: He's enabled us to share in an inheritance.

Doesn't that intrigue you? Don't you want to know what that inheritance is?

After all, an inheritance—depending on what it is—can completely change lives on this earth. If the Almighty has given me an inheritance, wouldn't that change my life in even more astonishing ways?

And before we go any further, let's note one key difference between an earthly inheritance and the inheritance God has for us. In this earthly life, if we expect an inheritance from another person, it means we *might* receive *something, someday.* Nothing is certain (because we know things may change), and in most cases, we have to wait to receive our inheritance until certain conditions are met.

Not so with the heavenly Father's gifts for His children. True, we cannot experience it all here and now. There is so much more being kept in heaven for us, where we finally will realize fully what it means to be called *son* or *daughter* of the Almighty Creator. But there's also a great deal of this inheritance that God has poured into our lives already. We can already live as heirs of the King. We are here and now receiving heavenly blessings and resources for our earthly journeys.

It's not a Cinderella story, not a fairy tale. It is the place of privilege where Christ has brought us. We are already living on the inheritance God lavishes on His children.

Yes. He *lavishes* His good gifts on us. Pick up any dictionary, and you'll find the definition of lavish is breathtaking; it means generous, heaped on, sumptuously rich, giving more than is necessary, profuse. I like this phrase from Merriam-Webster: *pouring forth without restraint.*

God has a vast storehouse of good gifts for those who come to Him.

That's part of our inheritance, and it pours into our lives daily.

MORE: Psalm 31:19; John 1:12; Galatians 4:7

KNOWING OUR INHERITANCE

No one can know a person's thoughts except that person's own spirit, and no one can know God's thoughts except God's own Spirit. And we have received God's Spirit (not the world's spirit), so we can know the wonderful things God has freely given us.

— 1 CORINTHIANS 2:11, 12 —

What exactly is this rich, generous, heaped up inheritance we're given today in this place of privilege?

God tells us.

He has not kept it secret. He doesn't make us guess or just go stumbling blindly through our days and hope we'll somehow discover our inheritance and fall into this living as a child of the King.

He has given us His Word to tell us, over and over and in many different ways and love languages, what He has for us. The Bible can change your life, child of God. It's His direct word to you, right here and now. Ask Him to make more of it plain to you. He is delighted to answer those prayers.

His Word also came into the world as a human, to relate to us on a human level. Jesus said if we get to know Him, we are also getting to know the Father. He came to show us God.

And God did something else that amazes me. "He has identified us as his own by placing the Holy Spirit in our hearts" (2 Corinthians 1:22). His Spirit lives in His children! This is essential for our connection to our Creator. Throughout the following chapters, we'll see more and more of how the Spirit works in our lives, but for now, I'd like to point you to the verse opening this meditation. Take a moment to read it if you haven't already...

What a place of privilege! We have been given a connection to God's own thoughts. God's Spirit within us helps us to know Him. And the Spirit within also helps us to see and understand "the wonderful things God has freely given us." I believe those wonderful things include our inheritance as children of God, and in the following pages, we'll explore many parts of that inheritance.

We do stand in a privileged place as children of the heavenly Father. From where we now stand, we look back at our past and know that we are not prisoners of whatever has gone before—all of that is in His hands. He heals, forgives, and has cleared our record. We stand in this spot and know that we can live today with the resources God pours into our lives. And as we look toward the future, we'll see that this inheritance God has given us will never run out. It will not be depleted as we go forward into tomorrow. We can never get to the end of the goodness He has for us. There is no quota on what you can draw from the resources He gives us. It will not be rescinded.

As a matter of fact, the more we begin to live like children of the King, the more we'll realize and experience what life in His Kingdom is all about.

And if you're getting impatient, wondering what, exactly and specifically, your inheritance is, be patient. We're getting there.

On second thought, go ahead. Go straight to God's Word and Jesus and the Holy Spirit already working in your heart and ask to be shown more of the wonderful things He has given you. I don't mind at all.

MORE:1 Corinthians 2:9, 10; Galatians 3:26; Ephesians 1:18

 LIVING IN HEAVEN'S REALITIES

For the Kingdom of God is not just a lot of talk;
it is living by God's power.
- 1 CORINTHIANS 4:20 -

I'm a Maine-iac. Almost two decades ago, I fell in love with a state. I still live a thousand miles away, but if I see the word *Maine* or *Lubec,* my thoughts and emotions are immediately transported to another place, an environment, an atmosphere, a way of thinking, a feeling, a sense of community.

Where does the word *heaven* take you? When you see the word, do your thoughts and emotions go to a someday, somewhere in the future?

Let's change that.

Let's change our thinking about heaven—not because we don't want to think about heaven, but because heaven is not limited to something far off in the future. We are already living in the heavenly kingdom and its realities.

Paul wrote in Ephesians 2:6 that when God gave us a new life, He "seated us with him (Christ) in the heavenly realms." Now, you are sitting in your chair, reading this book. You aren't in "heaven"—that future, perfect place—yet, are you? What could that verse mean?

It means that we are already living in God's Kingdom, in a spiritual realm, in realities beyond earthly realities. Life here is quite different than in the "realities" of the world.

Yes, we are still on this earth, traveling through this life in this world. But our citizenship is elsewhere. And in that realm where our citizenship lies, the King has declared we are His children and heirs. Much of our inheritance awaits us there when we will finally come into our full rights as His children. But our Father is already giving us access to the blessings and resources of our inheritance as we travel on toward home.

What are those blessings? We find some of them listed in the opening of Paul's letter to the believers in Colosse. We have access to:

- The knowledge of God's will
- Spiritual wisdom and understanding
- Strength, endurance, and patience that come from God's incredible, great power
- Joy
- Sharing in everything God has for His people
- Freedom from the kingdom of darkness
- Forgiveness of our sins

(all from Colossians 1:9-14)

Oh! That could be the outline for another seven books!

Living in the Kingdom of God. Living as children of God. It's not just a lot of talk, as Paul wrote in 1 Corinthians 4:20. It's living by God's power, living according to what God says we are and have as His children.

God says we stand in a place of great privilege. He says heavenly resources are available to us. It's not just a lot of talk. It's putting our hope in the Lord, the one who holds us and the future in His hands.

This affects *everything* about how we face tomorrow. In the years of the early church, Scriptures tell us that the Good News of God's gracious gifts to believers was building people up and changing lives everywhere (Acts 20:32, Colossians 1:6). Our lives, too, will be built up and changed as we learn and understand the truths of God's reality.

Let's get our feet under us, so to speak, and take

a firm stance as we turn toward the road ahead. Don't blindly follow the GPS commands of daily busyness, routines, and even religious traditions. Instead, know where you are as you head into the future. You're already living in the realm of heaven, standing in a place of great privilege. Ask the Spirit to show you all the good things God has for you and all the things He will do. Ask to see God's power. Ask for hope that will help you go confidently and joyfully toward tomorrow!

MORE: John 5:24; Ephesians 1:3, 18-20; 2 Peter 1:3, 4

⟣ HOW WE LIVE IN HEAVEN'S REALITIES ⟣

For we live by believing and not by seeing.
- 2 CORINTHIANS 5:7 -

"Live in heaven's realities."

Does that just seem like a lot of talk to you? Is it only a line of Christian-ese that has no relevance to your life today in the realities of this world?

Because heaven is invisible and intangible, it might often be difficult to think about living in those realms. But let's talk about the *invisible* realities of our lives as citizens of heaven and children of God.

Hebrews 11 uses an interesting image. Verse 27

says that Moses did not fear the king's anger when he led the people of Israel out of Egypt. "He kept right on going because he kept his eyes on the one who is invisible."

Can we say the same about our own lives? In spite of opposition, disappointment, setbacks, and the enemy constantly trying to poison us with doubt, do we keep right on going because our eyes are on God? We often falter. At least, I know that I do.

After all, how do we keep our eyes on something that is invisible?

We need eyes of faith.

Another example. In Paul's letter to Timothy, he wrote of "taking hold" of eternal life (1 Timothy 6:12 NIV). Hold on to it tightly, he advised. This might seem just as impossible as "seeing" someone who is invisible! How do we take hold of eternal life right now?

Paul certainly didn't mean that we can achieve eternal life by our own abilities or grab it by our own efforts. Immortality comes only as a gift from the kindness of God. What Paul does mean is that we've been given the gift, and now we need to live it. Live like children of the King, live in heavenly realities, and see the things that are invisible!

We need something specific to guide us, don't we?

The One who is invisible has given us loving

IN A PLACE OF PRIVILEGE

instructions, showing us how to move through this earthly life while living according to heavenly realities. His instructions come in the form of concrete promises, and when we build our day-to-day living on what He says we can depend on and expect, then we are keeping our eyes of faith on Him. When our perspective, decisions, and actions are guided by His promises, we are putting all our hope in Him.

The Greek and Hebrew words that we have translated as hope in the Scriptures are *elpis* (Greek) and *yakhal* (Hebrew). Both of these words hold an expectation, a *knowing* that what is promised will happen. Our hope is much more than wishful thinking. Our hope knows. It expects. It sees what will happen because it is certain God will do what He says He will do.

Think of God's promises as bridges. The purpose of bridges is to provide a way to move ahead when faced with challenges in the road. Bridges carry us safely from one spot to the next when we might otherwise be brought to a halt in our journey. God's promises are like that. We know the bridges of promise He has built for us will hold true and carry us, so we cross, safely and confidently moving ahead because we trust the One who built the bridge to help us in our journey.

We take hold of eternal life—yes, we live our

eternal lives right now—as we learn to live according to His promises. That's how we live in heaven's realities.

So it's a good thing to know God's promises to us. We cannot see into the future, but we know His promises will be there to help us, and we can depend on them to carry us. As we stand on the brink of the next hour, the next day, the next year, we can live with great hope because we know He will keep His word. He doesn't lie. He doesn't pull the rug out from under us and change His mind every now and then. Again and again, He gives us assurances of who He is and what He will do.

Our hope can *know*.

That's what we want to do and where we want to go in the following pages. We want to discover more of what God has promised His children, take hold of this eternal life He's given us, and live from our place of privilege. We want to be able to face the future with the confidence that the bridges God has put before us are trustworthy.

MORE: Psalm 119:114; 1 Timothy 6:12; Hebrews 10:23

PRAYER FOR MORE TASTES OF THE POWER:

Open my eyes to see your wonderful truths.

– **PSALM 119:18 AP** –

TASTING THE POWER

 TASTE OF HEAVENLY THINGS

Taste and see that the LORD is good.
Oh, the joys of those who take refuge in him!

- **PSALM 34:8** -

One year, my friends and I vacationed in Maine when the trees were showing off their finest October splendor. Never before had we seen such beautiful autumn colors—reds, oranges, and golds blazing in sunshine or glowing like embers in the mist and fog.

Having coffee with a native Mainer one day, I mentioned our delight at having the good fortune to witness this exceptional color.

"Oh," she said, "this is nothing compared to what it can be."

It could be even more beautiful than what we were seeing? Her words lit a longing in me. Someday, I thought, I want to see "what it can be."

Even more intense is a longing that rises when I read the apostle Paul's words of tasting "the power of the age to come."

Let that phrase sink into your soul.

The words are from Hebrews 6:5. The context of the words is a warning about the terrible condition of someone who has once believed, who has "experienced the good things of heaven and shared in the Holy Spirit, who [has] tasted the goodness of... God and the power of the age to come" and then turns his back on God.

It is not the warning we want to focus on now, but this fact: In this life, we have a taste of the good things of heaven!

Yes. We have a sampling of heaven in the here and now. You often hear something described as "heaven on earth." The words are often spoken lightly—but the next time you hear them, remember that we can indeed experience a bit of the real heaven while we are here on earth.

The power of the heavenly realm is not only something we will know someday in a new life. It is already here, active and vigorous, in the life we live today. We see it in every promise God has made to us. He is always working—even in this very moment—to bring about His eternal, heavenly plans. As we face the future, God's kindness gives our hope tastes of what He will provide for us when His plan is fully accomplished.

One example is the beauty in nature. There have been days so glorious, so perfect, that I've questioned how any world could be more beautiful. Then I sometimes hear my heavenly Father say, "Oh, daughter, just wait till you see your new world!" I've been in natural settings so awe-inspiring that the beauty calls forth an ache, and I wonder if the ache is something eternal inside me, something that knows, without my consciousness of it, that full, unblemished beauty is waiting for me—and the eternal within me longs to be there.

Another example is that God intends to live with His people. Always. Fully. His presence will always be with us. We don't have to wait for life after our earthly death to experience the goodness of God's presence. He lives with us now. He is interacting with us now, giving us tastes of His goodness, even while we're still walking this planet.

Revelation 21:4 promises that God will wipe away all sorrow and crying and pain. Although that gift of the loving Father will be complete in heaven, He is not reserving all of the blessing until then.

His presence, compassion, and healing are already working in our lives.

More tastes: Psalm 23. As we experience our Shepherd's provision for our needs while we are still on this earth, we have a small taste of what heaven's abundant resources will provide. We read in Revelation 7:17 that Jesus will be our Shepherd forever. Each of those verses in Psalm 23 will be realized fully and perfectly in our final home. For example, the seasons of rest and green pastures now are a taste of the perfect rest coming someday.

And one more example: Someday, we will be transformed completely to bear the image of God we were first intended to have. But God is not waiting until "someday" to make us like Him. He has already begun the process of changing us through the teaching and molding of the Holy Spirit (see 2 Corinthians 3:18).

We are given a taste of the good things of heaven. Not experiencing them fully and perfectly, but tasting, *partaking of,* the power of the future. I think God has given us these tastes of what is to come because He wants us to know the great storehouses of goodness He has for us. He wants us to look ahead eagerly. Our eternal life has already begun, and He wants our hearts to be hungry for even more of this relationship with Him.

We have tastes of the future God has planned

for us. Expect them every day. And know that this is only a taste. Wait until you see what it all *will* be!

MORE: Psalm 23:6; Psalm 27:4; Ecclesiastes 3:11

 **GUARANTEE**

And he has identified us as his own by placing the Holy Spirit in our hearts as the first installment that guarantees everything he has promised us.

– **2 CORINTHIANS 1:22** –

Isn't it amazing that the Almighty Creator, Lord of the Universe, has given us the gift of eternal life? And by eternal life, I am not referring to life that goes on after death. I'm referring to life in eternal, heavenly dimensions right now. He has opened heaven to pour heaven's blessings and resources into our earthly lives. Eternity has come into the time-bound. Heavenly has come into the earthly.

It's a difficult thing to comprehend and believe because our "earthliness" so confines us. We might think we're limited by what we can see and touch and feel—but we are not! We have eyes that can see the invisible, we can taste the power of the eternal, and we can hear what the Spirit speaks to us. We can know even what earthly minds cannot prove.

And above all else, we have God's guarantee.

God guarantees that one day, we will have not just tastes but the fullness and completeness of what He's planned for His children. The Holy Spirit, His presence living right here in us, is the "first installment" of what God has for His heirs.

Is it difficult to believe the Spirit of God lives in you?

With the gift of the Spirit, God says, "This is the seal that you are my child." We readily accept that children born of earthly parents carry their parents' traits. We say things like "She has her mother's spirit of adventure" or "That entrepreneurial spirit seems to run in the family." Believer, follower of Jesus Christ, child of God, know that this new life you're living was birthed by God. And His Spirit does live in you.

That's actually one of the ways in which the Spirit is our "Comforter"—He assures us that we are indeed children of God (Romans 8:16). If you need more confidence in this, ask for more! Our heavenly Father will give it to you.

With this declaration of our new status as children of God comes the promise of an inheritance, a granting of all the rights, privileges, and resources due His sons and daughters. Scripture even says we are co-heirs with Christ (Romans 8:17).

Our full inheritance will come later and will be beyond anything we can imagine. But we already have a taste of what is coming. The Holy Spirit is God working in us right now. He is our special connection to God, His thoughts, and His character. The Spirit in us teaches, guides, strengthens, advises, and comforts. He is always present with us, and always working. His work draws us ever closer to our Creator Father.

The Holy Spirit is the seal God has given, pledging that the tastes we have now will one day be the full-blown fulfillment of all His promises.

You know, God could have created the world and then stepped back and let it spin on, chugging along to whatever destiny it brought on itself. But He did not do so. He has plans for this earth and its people. He could have demanded worship and obedience as some absent deity, withdrawn from the world but still holding our future in His hands. He did not do that, either, but is intimately involved in the lives of His people, living right here with us. And I believe He has given us these tastes of what is to come to encourage us. He's giving us glimpses of the future— and it is *His* future into which we will walk, not just some random, coincidental one. His promises give us assurance as we go forward.

His Holy Spirit is the guarantee of all He has promised. As we face the future, the Creator Father wants us to know He is committed to His children.

MORE: Romans 8:16; 2 Corinthians 5:5; Ephesians 1:13-14

 ANCHORED

This hope is a strong and trustworthy anchor for our souls.
- **HEBREWS 6:19** -

The bright colors of the lobster boats shone in the afternoon sunshine. As a strong ebb tide pulled insistently, the boats rocked in the wind and strained against the taut lines securing them to their mooring.

The friendly man at the information center looked out over the bay, and his tanned, weathered face broke into a grin as he told one of his favorite stories about people "from away." He had lived in this little seaside village all his life, and in recent years, vacationers had discovered the town.

"Yup," he nodded. "I get lots of interesting questions here. I once had a woman ask me how they managed to get all those boats parked in the same direction."

Of course, that was just the natural effect of the wind and current turning the boats about, attempting to pull them away. I smiled at the man's story but was thinking about those boats, held steady by one line. If it were not for their attachment to strong moorings, they would be at the mercy of the elements. Loose on the tides and blown about, they would be in danger of crashing on the rocky shore or being swept away toward the Atlantic Ocean—if they did not sink first.

We, too, need a strong mooring to hold us steady.

Who knows what the wind and tides of the future will attempt to do to our boats?

We have prophecies about the future. But even the people who were inspired to give us those messages did not understand everything God had told them to say.

Because prophecy attempts to explain matters not yet part of our experience, we can easily get tangled in debates on the meaning of symbols, the sequence and duration of God's timeline, and the identity of key players in the events of this world's last breaths. We end up with confused and contradictory interpretations. This is not unique to our day. Even among those who diligently studied the prophecies about the coming of a Messiah, only a few recognized Him when He did arrive as a baby in Bethlehem.

Jesus said the timing of everything God has planned is not for us to know. Only the Father knows the schedule. Nevertheless, many try to sort out all the details and even predict dates when certain events will happen.

Some prophetic words—such as the prophecies about the coming of Jesus and all nations being invited to become God's children—have already been fulfilled. Many people are convinced that prophecies about the end times of this earth are now playing out on the world's stage. More prophecies about the new earth and Christ's rule have yet to come to pass.

I am not a scholar of Biblical prophecy or the end times. I believe, though, that even the most persistent and focused student of prophecy has only a glimpse of all God has planned for the creation He loves. I believe the unfolding of His plans will surprise us. Even though we are admonished to be watchful and ready, God's plans go far beyond what we can imagine.

We cannot distinctly see what is to come, but God has given us encouraging glimpses of the future because He wants us to know He has good plans. He wants us to know He is the rock, the refuge we can always count on.

We taste the power of the age to come as we build our lives on the promises of God. While there are many Scripture passages about the future that remain a mystery, we can be certain of God's promises, given to us in clear language. Those promises hold wonderful tastes of heavenly power and blessings, which we can have now.

God's promises are the focus of this book. Not prophecy. Not debate on timelines, symbolism, and players on the stage of the last days of this earth. We want, instead, to hear and celebrate what God has promised His children. We want to know and claim the comfort in Scriptures that speak peace to our hearts and minds as we wonder about what is coming tomorrow and how we will be able to walk through it.

We want to anchor our hope in those promises so we aren't blown to devastation by anything coming tomorrow, next year, or in the decades that follow.

MORE: Psalm 73:26; Psalm 119:165; Romans 5:5

🌿 GREAT CONFIDENCE 🌿

Therefore, we who have fled to him for refuge can have
great confidence as we hold to the hope that lies before us.
- **HEBREWS 6:18** -

You can have great confidence as you face tomorrow.

I want to live with great confidence. I don't want to be frozen by fear and wearied by worry. How about you?

The verse above from Hebrews gives us two keys to such living.

First, this great confidence comes to those who go to the Lord for refuge. The living God provides us with a refuge from the fear and worry. (And isn't that a welcome relief from our fretting?) Those who put their trust in God will have peace, be filled with hope, will find strength, and will not be disappointed or defeated. We looked at these promises in the first chapter. Go back to that meditation if you want to be reminded of what God has to say.

The second key we have here is that confidence comes when we hold to the hope. What is that hope? To hold on to the hope, we'll need to know exactly what God has promised—and that's what this book is about.

The verse begins with the word *Therefore*. This tells us something has been stated previously, something which leads to this conclusion. In the verses preceding verse 18, the writer of Hebrews explained that God made it perfectly clear His promise would not change, and He guaranteed the promise with an oath. James wrote that God does not change like "shifting shadows" (James 1:17). We can be confident God is not playing games with us. He doesn't try to be elusive and hard to pin down. He says plainly and unmistakably what He will do so our hope can know and we can depend on Him.

Then, we hold to the hope when we base our living on those promises. We think and act accordingly because we know what God has said He will do. It's not just wishful thinking. We expect it. Our eyes of faith can "see" it. Our hope knows the fulfillment of these promises lies ahead.

All of us have at some time tried to stabilize our boats by holding on to things other than God and His promises. And we have found that other "hopes," other anchors, fail us. They disappoint. They do not hold us steady. We cannot rely on them through either the storm or the quiet waters.

We want to stand firm.

Our heavenly Father brings His blessings and power into our earthly lives so we can do just that.

MORE: Psalm 20:7, 8; Psalm 31:24; 2 Corinthians 1:8-10

 LIVE WITH GREAT EXPECTATION!

Now we live with great expectation.

- 1 PETER 1:3 -

What might happen if we made the above words our rallying cry? What if we used that title to encourage each other as we journey together through this life?

Is it realistic?

Again, let's ask ourselves whether we want to live according to the world's view of "realistic" or according to God's.

According to God's view, we can live with great expectation. Remember the meaning of hope: a confidence that something promised will happen.

The statement from 1 Peter 1:3 comes from a passage with many wonderful assurances. May I summarize? Then you might want to take the time to read it for yourself and tuck the promises away in your heart and mind. It will increase your peace! As a matter of fact, the passage is preceded by those words, "May God give you more and more grace and peace."

Here are comforts from the nine opening verses of Peter's first letter:

God's great mercy has given you a new life, a life that will go on forever, and this life is one with great expectation. You've been given an inheritance, one that will not dwindle away or be taken from you. As you journey on toward heaven, "God is protecting you by his power" because of your faith.

"So be truly glad," wrote Peter. "There is wonderful joy ahead." Even though the road may be rough. Even though you have never seen the One you trust. Yet, loving and trusting Him will bring a "glorious, inexpressible joy." (There's that promise of joy again.)

And if you trust Him, your soul will be rescued, both now and on into forever.

Does your soul need rescue? Mine does, on a daily basis. And I know I'll need His rescue often as I go forward into whatever is waiting down the road. But as we trust His promises, we can live with great expectation.

Let's do it!

There is wonderful joy ahead.

MORE: *John 14:1; 2 Thessalonians 2:16, 17; 2 Peter 1:3, 4*

〜 CALLING FOR HELP 〜

"LORD, help!" they cried in their trouble, and he rescued
them from their distress.
− **PSALM 107:6** −

Maybe you see little hope in your life right now. Maybe all that is in view on the horizon is an ominous gathering of storm clouds. Perhaps your boat is already rocking violently, and your line to your anchor looks much too thin and fragile to hold you steady.

May I suggest three things?

First, read Psalm 107. My story is there, and I'm guessing you will see yourself somewhere there, too. The chapter is a series of accounts of people in many distressing situations—some of those situations were brought about by their own unwise choices—who asked God for help. God's answer was always rescue. He heard their cries for help and rescued them from their distress.

The psalm begins and ends with thankfulness: *Give thanks to the Lord, because He is good to us. His love goes on forever.*

He is good. His love for you never fades, is never withdrawn. Whatever your circumstances are now, whatever situation is looming in your future and worrying you, He knows about it and cares about you having to walk through it.

So, secondly, ask Him for help. Ask Him to strengthen your hope. Ask for peace and confidence. Ask for the comfort of knowing you are His child. He hears and answers those prayers! And our hope grows as our relationship with our Father grows.

Have you noticed each chapter here begins with a prayer? These are meant to help our hope. They are all from the book of Psalms; David, a man who had a great deal of turmoil and trouble in his life, wrote most of them. He knew all the ups and downs of trust in God. There were times David exulted in God's nearness and blessing but also times that he doubted God even cared about what was happening. Yet God declared that David's heart was in tune with His own.

We have the same ups and downs. We have some of the same joys and doubts, so I've pulled some of David's heartfelt prayers to help us in our own praying. They're short and easy to memorize. Use them as your own when you need encouragement and help from your heavenly Father.

Thirdly, read God's words to you. Every time you sit down to read the Scriptures, you can ask Him for a direct word. The Holy Spirit will connect you to the Father, and you'll be comforted, encouraged, and helped—whatever you need each day for your hope to grow so you can keep walking forward in confidence.

Through your prayers and listening to His Word, you'll be building your relationship with your heavenly Father. And your hope will be tasting the blessings of heaven and the power of the age to come.

MORE: Psalm 50:15; Jeremiah 33:3; Hebrews 6:17-19

PRAYER FOR OUR JOURNEY:

I know you are always with me. I will not be shaken, for you are right beside me. I rejoice in that, and my heart is glad.

— **PSALM 16:8, 9 AP** —

WE AREN'T
TRAVELING ALONE

∽ NEVER ALONE ∾

You go before me and follow me.
You place your hand of blessing on my head.

- **PSALM 139:5** -

The loneliest time of your life.

I'm guessing those six words immediately take you back to a specific situation. Maybe fragments of feelings still linger from that desolate time and suddenly well up inside you now. What were you facing then?

It may have been the loneliest time of your life, but you were not alone.

As we stand at the edge of today, poised to step into the future, our hope can know that we do not have to take even one small step alone. From the very first day that God created man and woman, He has been present and working in His people's lives, and tomorrow He will be present and working in our lives, too.

Isn't that amazing? The Almighty Creator, the Lord of the Universe, will be traveling the road with us. David knew this. In Psalm 139, he tried to describe it: the Lord, surrounding David with His presence, walking the road ahead, following behind, and continually keeping His hand of blessing on him. Various translations use different words: *hemmed in, encircled, hedged in, enclosed, all around me.* Do you get the sense of being surrounded by God's protective love?

You might think David was special, a favorite child of the heavenly Father. They did, after all, have an intense, strong relationship. But David's experience of God's constant presence in his life is what God has been doing all along, ever since He brought humankind into existence—and what He will be doing in each of our journeys into the unknown future. No matter where the road goes, "even there your hand will guide me and your strength will support me" (Psalm 139:10).

We can't read the Bible through without hearing

God say, again and again, *I am here. I will be your God. I will help you and show you the way to real life.*

Many of the Biblical accounts have parallels for our lives as we face tomorrow. We know that our God is the same God we find in the Bible, so let's take a look at what God says to us as we peer ahead and wonder what the future might bring.

MORE: Psalm 145:18; Lamentations 3:57; Acts 17:27

GOD AMONG HIS PEOPLE

For your presence among us sets your people and me apart from all other people on the earth.

‒ **EXODUS 33:16** ‒

In some ways, Moses was just like you and me.

Can you identify with Moses' reluctance when God gave him a job that looked impossible? Moses had excuses. *No one will believe me. I'm not capable. Someone else could do it better.* I'm sure that underlying all those excuses was the thought that what God was planning could never happen. It just wasn't possible. God had even told Moses there would be strong resistance to the plan.

I admit that I've had doubts and expressed some of those same feelings to God.

Standing in front of the burning bush, Moses heard God explain what He had in mind. Moses was given the plan for his future, but he just couldn't see it. How could this possibly happen? At least three times God reassured Moses: "I will be with you." And still, Moses felt uneasy.

Let's not be too hard on Moses—we, too, have had our reservations about moving into a risky, dangerous future.

By the time Moses utters the words that open this meditation, he and the Israelites have left Egypt and are in the Sinai desert. Moses has seen many astounding acts of the Almighty who has, indeed, brought the Israelites out of Egypt. That in itself was a miraculous event. He has also seen the plagues, the crossing of the Red Sea, the meeting with God on the mountain, the promise that God would supply food and water and protection along the way, and the assurance that God would go ahead of them and defeat their enemies in advance. The pillar of cloud and the pillar of fire, God's presence guiding the Israelites, never left them. Scripture even tells us that the Lord would speak to Moses face to face.

Yet the day came when Moses wanted even more reassurance of God's presence with them. He wanted to "see" more and to understand more fully.

Was this request merely an inability to fully

understand God's commitment to always being present with us? Or was it Moses' expression of how completely he depended on God being with them? I think it may have been the latter. Moses knew God's presence was essential. Unless God went with them, their journey through the wilderness would be futile. They would never find or take their Promised Land. They would not survive. "If you don't personally go with us," he told God, "then don't even ask us to go one step further" (Exodus 33:15 AP).

How patient God was with Moses! He had shown His commitment to the Israelites in so many powerful ways, but He did not scold Moses for wanting more reassurance. He repeated His promise. "I will go with you."

How patient God is with us! He has done many great things for us—He rescued us from slavery in our own "Egypt," freed us, and said, "I want to be your God." He has promised to take care of our needs, to guide us, and to always be with us. Yet sometimes we doubt, we question, and we wonder how His promises could possibly come to completion.

In answer to the request, God gave Moses a glimpse of His glory that day. (See Exodus 33:12-23)

Years later, when Moses gave instructions to the Israelites as they prepared to enter the land of Canaan, he looked back at their long sojourn in the wilderness and reminded them, "[God] has watched your every step through this great wilderness. During these forty years, the LORD your God has been with you, and you have lacked nothing" (Deuteronomy 2:7). True, there were still battles ahead, and the people knew it. But Moses told them,

> So be strong and courageous! Do not be afraid and do not panic before them. For the LORD your God will personally go ahead of you. He will neither fail you nor abandon you. (Deuteronomy 31:6)

Centuries later, the writer of Hebrews reflected on Moses' life and his accomplishment of the tasks God gave Him. The secret was this: In spite of all opposition, Moses "kept right on going because he kept his eyes on the one who is invisible" (Hebrews 11:27).

As we look ahead, knowing there are battles, rough stretches of road, and enemies that lie in wait, our hope can know that the Lord will always go ahead of us and follow behind us. We do not need to panic as challenges loom ahead. When storms howl around us, or the enemy besieges our walls, our hope stands on His promises that He will not fail or abandon His children.

His constant presence with us is what gives us a hope that cannot be found or manufactured anywhere else.

And when we need more reassurance of His presence, we can ask Him for eyes to see the invisible—that He is always there.

MORE: Deuteronomy 20:1; Psalm 23:4; Haggai 2:4, 5; John 14:23

BELIEVE AND BE COURAGEOUS

This is my command—be strong and courageous!
Do not be afraid or discouraged.
For the LORD your God is with you wherever you go.
- JOSHUA 1:9 -

When Moses died, his assistant, Joshua, inherited the leadership role and the promises of God. In the opening verses of the book of Joshua, we hear God repeat His promises to Joshua: "I will always be with you, just as I was with Moses. I'm not going to abandon you. Don't be afraid. I will give you all that I've promised."

These are words we read in many Biblical accounts: "Don't be afraid. I am here. I will do exactly what I promised." And because our God is the same God who always walked with David, who gave Moses reassurance of His presence, and who told Joshua that He was still there and would not abandon him, we can also claim this promise.

Stop for a moment and consider the one thing that you fear most in the future...

Your hope can know this: God will be walking with you as you meet that thing you fear, and He will do everything He has said He will do as you walk through it.

You can depend on Him. If you read Joshua 1:1-9, you can't miss the firm declaration from God that Joshua could be strong and courageous because God would be right there with him. Joshua moved ahead, into the future, fighting the battles and taking the land God would give the Israelites.

We find a sad, contrasting account in Psalm 106, a chapter that looks back at the history of the Israelites. Verse 24 recalls the generation before Joshua, the generation who died in the wilderness and never entered the Promised Land. Why not? Because "[T]hey wouldn't believe [God's] promise to care for them."

There was that good land, "flowing with milk and honey," just across the river. It was the fulfillment of all their hopes. But in the end, the people did not believe God would or could make good on His promise. And so they never entered the land and missed all the blessings.

Know that God will never abandon you. Depend on it. And search God's Word so that you know what He has said He will do for you. Don't miss out by not trusting Him. The resources and blessings He will provide as you travel now are a small taste of everything that is to come—all the full blessings of heaven. Be strong and courageous. Depend on Him to keep those promises as you go forward with Him into the future, always heading onward toward our real Promised Land.

MORE: Isaiah 43:2; Psalm 33:4; Hebrews 13:5

 **HIS REASON**

And they will know that I am the LORD their God. I am the one who brought them out of the land of Egypt so that I could live among them.

- **EXODUS 29:46** -

Let's back up just a bit and look at the point at which God brought the Israelites out of slavery in Egypt and started them on their journey to another land.

The childhood Sunday School versions of what we call the Exodus never mentioned one detail. Or maybe it was mentioned and I never caught it before, but now it has become very important to me. I wonder if you noticed it when you read our opening verse.

My early understanding of the account of Israel's rescue was that God wanted to set His people free from the oppressive slavery and take them to a new land of their own. But during several years when I was doing a Bible read-through in four months—which requires concentrated times of reading more than just a chapter or two a day—a new theme emerged from the Old Testament passages. There was an additional layer of the story that I had not realized before: God wanted to live with His people and be their God.

We read it over and over. God wants to live with His people. First, He rescued them from Egypt so that He could be their God. Then He told Moses to build a tent sanctuary in the wilderness camp, a physical, visual reminder of His presence with them. After they were settled in their new land, a Temple was built, a building of stone and wood. We hear God saying throughout Israel's history that He would live with His people.

And He wanted to be their God.

Isn't our story much the same? God has rescued us from the kingdom of darkness, where we were prisoners and slaves. He has transferred us to His own kingdom and even adopted us as His heirs. He's claimed us as His own and says He will always live with us—to be our God.

The Almighty Creator wants to be your God. What does that mean to you?

Notice the Scriptures in our focus for this chapter. They promise God's presence with us all the days of our lives in this world, but they also tell us why His presence is so significant, so absolutely necessary for us. Here's a sampling:

- God's hand will guide me, and His strength will support me. (Psalm 139:10)

- I do not need to be afraid or discouraged because the Lord is with me. (Joshua 1:9)

- The Lord goes ahead of me and will not fail me or desert me. (Deuteronomy 31:6)

- God will strengthen and help me. He will hold me up in victory. (Isaiah 41:10)

- God watches over me. (Psalm 33:18)

- The Lord watches over my life—and never takes a break! (Psalm 121)

- The Lord, my Shepherd, supplies everything I need. (Psalm 23)

- The Lord rules over everything! (Psalm 103:19)

The list could go on and on. This is what God being God brings to our lives. Almost every reference to God being ever-present with us also holds promises of what He will be to us. Is it any wonder that Moses did not want to take one more step if God were not going with them?

He is God. He says there is no other, no one as glorious, no one as powerful, no one so worthy of being worshipped. He is God.

This only One worthy of worship wants to live with His people. Always and forever. He wants it to be personal—He wants to be our God.

MORE: Isaiah 46:4; Ezekiel 37:26, 27; Revelation 21:3, 4

GOD IN HIS TEMPLE

And when you believed in Christ, he identified you as his own by giving you the Holy Spirit, whom he promised long ago.

– EPHESIANS 1:13 –

God came to His people in the wilderness in a cloud and a pillar of fire. The fire and cloud were guidance, protection, and comfort for the homeless Israelites. Later, His presence filled the sanctuaries of the tent tabernacle and the Temple built in Jerusalem by human hands.

Then God's presence came to His people in Jesus Christ, a man who could identify with us and who came to show us who God is. Soon after Jesus' death, the Temple in Jerusalem was destroyed. But God was already at work building another temple for Himself among His people—you and me, and every believer who claims Christ as King.

God now dwells on earth in His Holy Spirit within believers. And He continues to be God to His people! He shepherds us through His Holy Spirit within us. Jesus' parting words to His followers give us the firm promise: God's Spirit will never leave us.

But we underestimate His presence with us.

It is through the Spirit that we taste more and more of heaven's power and blessings. He is always with us, and this is what He does for us:

- Leads us to truth. (John 14:17)

- Reminds us of what Jesus taught. (John 14:26)

- Tells us about the future. (John 16:13)

- Prays for us when we don't even have words to pray. (Romans 8:26)

- Gives us an understanding of God. (1 Corinthians 2:10-12)

- Changes and molds us into Christ's glorious image. (2 Corinthians 3:18)

- Helps us do the right thing. (Galatians 5:16)

- Produces good qualities in us. (Galatians 5:22-23)

- Gives us inner strength. (Ephesians 3:16)

- Gives us right desires and attitudes.
  (Ephesians 4:23)

As I travel through this life, I am in need of all those things. Is it any wonder that He is also referred to as the Comforter? All of these works of the Spirit point us toward our future destiny, the ultimate plans God has for us. And like Moses, we really can't go one more step into the future unless God's Holy Spirit goes with us.

And I'd like to point out one more amazing thing: the Spirit working in us is a taste of the power of what is to come.

> The Spirit of God, who raised Jesus from the dead, lives in you. And just as God raised Christ Jesus from the dead, he will give life to your mortal bodies by this same Spirit living within you. (Romans 8:11)

It is the Spirit—already in us—who is going to make us immortal!

May this be our prayer today: that our Father will give us a glimpse of the power of the Comforter who lives with us already and will always be with us.

MORE: John 14:16-18; 1 Corinthians 6:19; 1 John 4:4

SUPERNATURAL CONNECTION

I want them to be encouraged and knit
together by strong ties of love.
- **COLOSSIANS 2:2** -

The list we built of the things the Spirit does as He lives with us includes another thing: He gives us a supernatural connection to others who also belong to Christ.

Yes, we can use the word *supernatural* here because this relationship we have to other believers goes beyond the natural inclination that draws us to certain people and prompts us to avoid others. The bond we have with others in whom the Spirit dwells overrides all of those preferences and creates what God has called His living temple on earth.

You are part of the temple where God now resides in this world.

Jesus said He would "build" His church. Ephesians 2:22 tells us this building is an ongoing thing. We are "being built together" (NIV) into a place where God lives. That is encouraging to me. God is always at work. And in the times when we are disappointed in our congregation for whatever reason, I believe we can claim that promise that God is always working for our good—whether it is in us personally or in the church that Jesus is building. He hasn't waved his hand and created the perfect church instantly. Just as the Spirit has much work to do within me, He also has work to do within His church.

But back to God's plan for the church.

This unity with other believers (whether they are a part of our own congregation or not) is created as a gift of the Spirit for our growth, protection, comfort, and encouragement. In the opening verse, the love that Paul's prayer asks for the church is the same love and unity that Jesus prayed for His followers to have (John 17:23). This was a matter of intense prayer for Jesus.

Since our bond is created by the one Spirit we share and the one King we follow, we can encourage each other. Especially now, as we face the future, the word *encourage* means much more to me than to simply give someone a boost or cheer them up.

Look at the word closely. The prefix *en-* is used to indicate "in, into, or inside." To encourage is to nurture courage in someone else. 1 Thessalonians 5:11 tells us to encourage each other and build each other up. Don't we all need more courage as we face the future? The phrase "building each other up" gives us a vision of strengthening, bolstering, and making more solid. We have the power to do that in other believers' lives.

Are you thinking, *Encouraging and building up others? Me? I'm not sure I know how to do that.*

Yes. You. And me. And every believer. We do have "what it takes" to bolster each other's courage and faith. The Holy Spirit is at work equipping the church. He has given everyone a gift, and we are to "use them well to serve one another" (1 Peter 4:10). These are gifts that operate in the spiritual realm. They are meant to strengthen us, both as individuals and as the church.

Christ, at the head of His body, also intends to use the church for our protection—we'll delve into that more in another chapter.

We are an interesting mix of people in this family. Our hope knows that we have a supernatural connection with others who can and will help us along our journey. And we, in turn, are to help our sisters and brothers. None of God's children travel alone.

MORE: Romans 12:6-10; 2 Timothy 2:22

~ DEPENDING ON HIM ~

Trust in the LORD with all your heart; do not depend on your own understanding. Seek his will in all you do, and he will show you which path to take.

- **PROVERBS 3:5, 6** -

All of our hope for this life is based on God's presence in the lives of His children and on His being our God.

I sometimes try to imagine what my life might be like if I had no hope in God. For example, what if I believe death is the end and I will simply cease to exist? Or what if I believe I must do everything on my own strength and wisdom? It might be a worthwhile exercise to imagine your life without any of the hope God gives. We start to realize, then, how much we depend on our God.

He has said He will supply all that we need. One of the Hope Knows books is based entirely on how God helps us get through today. We depend on Him for everything, but I'd like to look at just one of those things that has been so important in my own life— His guidance.

The following story is almost too embarrassing to tell. I won't use the names of the two friends who were with me, so they, at least, do not have to be red-faced once the world learns what we did.

On our way to New England, we stopped at a bed and breakfast in Massachusetts. I'd read about Tyringham Cobble, a small state park just across the street from our lodging. A two-mile loop trail wound up and around the hill and through the woods, connecting at one point with a short stretch of the Appalachian Trail. I wanted to walk that short loop. Besides the promise of a lovely walk through field and forest, we could say we'd actually walked on that famous trail!

So in the morning, three of us set off for our little walk. That's what we were prepared for—"a little walk." We didn't carry water, cell phones, or maps. Oh, we did check a map posted on the board at the trailhead. Yes, it was just a simple loop around the hill. Easy.

Off we went.

And we went... and went... and went...

As a matter of fact, we "went" so long that the one person who had chosen to stay back at the bed and breakfast was at the point of calling the police and reporting us as missing.

I don't know what happened that day. How could two miles take so long? How could we have gone wrong? Other trails crisscrossed ours, but we "thought" we stayed on the right path. At one place, we must have been on the Appalachian Trail because a sign said "Maine" with an arrow pointing one way and "Georgia" with an arrow in the opposite direction. But by that time, it was no cause for celebration. Might we truly end up in Georgia? It felt as though we'd walked that far. Or were we headed north? We had no idea. Blazes on trees pointed the way, but we weren't always certain what the blazes meant. At one point, we came out on a ridge with a beautiful view—but no sight of any buildings or roads, least of all our destination.

How could we possibly be *lost?* Surely we

were not. We were just going around a small hill... weren't we? We joked about the local paper back home headlining the story in a few days: SEARCH CONTINUES FOR LOCAL WOMEN STILL LOST ON TWO-MILE TRAIL. The apprehension was rising, though, in spite of the jokes.

Who knows how many times we took a wrong turn or went in circles? We kept walking, never sure exactly where we were. Eventually, we stumbled onto the path that led down the hill to the B&B.

All the emotions of that morning come back to me sometimes when I am faced with a decision and haven't a clue which way is the best way to go. *Which path should I take? And will I be going in the right direction?*

The One who has promised to always be with us, though, knows the best way. And we have many promises that He will guide us along that way.

Let's face it; we are prone to be unprepared, unwise, and unknowing. Especially so, since we can't see into the future. We are traveling an unknown trail. Oh, yes, we try to predict and control the future. But we can't. None of us can even know what will happen one hour from now.

This can be cause for great anxiety. Worry about tomorrow can eat holes in us, so that we completely lose any joys, blessings, and energy of today. And the enemy who wants to destroy our peace, our relationships, and especially our faith and courage wins a little bit of ground when he whispers fear about tomorrow. Yes, the enemy is lurking along the path, prepared to ambush you with grim predictions of what is around the bend.

Our hope can know this: The God who lives with His people has said He will lead us along the best paths for our lives.

Even when we can't see the path clearly or don't know how to read the blazes, His promise holds. I've been at those crossroads, when I have no way of knowing which direction is best. Then my hope goes to Psalm 32:8, and I remind God, *Father, you have promised!* And I believe that just as the Holy Spirit prays for us when we don't know how to pray for ourselves, His Spirit also guides my choice of a path when I can't see clearly.

Or we may be on the wrong path and not be aware of our error. We may have taken a wrong turn, or we may unknowingly be going around in circles. Then the Spirit also works to get us going in the right direction. Jesus is always with those who belong to Him.

We aren't traveling alone. And we can say, like Moses, that we don't want to go one more step without Him. His presence is absolutely necessary as we head off into the future.

MORE: *Psalm 32:8; Psalm 48:14; Isaiah 41:13*

⁓ ON THE PATH ⁓

Lead me along the path of everlasting life.

– PSALM 139:24 –

"Ah... what a life!"

I've said that. Haven't you?

Maybe it's said in envy of someone who has five weeks of vacation. Or is retired. Or has a weekly housekeeper. Or has the resources to travel extensively. Or...

You can fill in any picture you want to end that sentence. We tend to look at lives that are different from ours and think if we only had *that—now, that would be the life!*

But many of us have eventually found, earned, or otherwise obtained the thing we once envied—and we discovered it did not create the life we wanted.

We started this chapter feeling very much alone. Have you, along the way, found a bit of the joy David talks about in Psalm 21:6? I've replaced the pronoun referring to David to make this personal:

> You have endowed me with eternal blessings
> and given me the joy of your presence.

Has something of the joy of God's constant presence begun to flow through you? Does peace seem possible, as you stand on the threshold of the future?

Joy and *peace*. Those words are plastered everywhere during the Christmas season. But they are found only in one place: God's presence. We've been looking at Scripture that tells us of God's desire and promise to live with His people. Now let's talk about our desire to live with Him—because it is His presence that will bring everything we long for in life.

Consider the picture of life captured in each of these verses:

- David wrote that the one thing he asked of the Lord, the one thing he wanted most, was to "live in the house of the LORD all the days of my life." (Psalm 27:4)

- God is the fountain of life. (Psalm 36:9)

- "For they are transplanted to the LORD's own house. They flourish in the courts of our God. Even in old age they will still produce fruit; they will remain vital and green." (Psalm 92:13, 14)

- The Lord teaches us what is good for us and leads us along the right paths. If we listen to Him, peace will flow like a gentle river. (Isaiah 48:17, 18)

- The fruit of the Spirit includes peace and joy, and "letting the Spirit control your life leads to life and peace." (Galatians 5:22, 23, Romans 8:6)

There are many images here: being transplanted into the house of the Lord, flourishing in His courts, access to the fountain of life, being led along the path of life, peace like a river, peace and joy appearing in your life like fruit on a tree. Which image speaks most strongly to your soul? Choose it and carry it in your mind. "See" it with your eyes of faith.

Life. Joy. Peace. In the house of the Lord. We're there now, already enjoying His presence with us. God is not waiting until "someday." We already have a taste of the joys and pleasures of God living with His people.

My choice of the above images? "Flourishing in His courts." I want that! Ah... what a life!

MORE: Psalm 16:11; Psalm 63:1, 2; John 10:10

PRAYER TO KNOW MORE OF GOD'S LOVE:

Show me your unfailing love

in wonderful ways.

– **PSALM 17:7** –

WE'RE VERY
PRECIOUS TO HIM

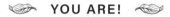

YOU ARE!

"Don't be afraid," he said, "for you are very precious to God.
Peace! Be encouraged! Be strong!"

– DANIEL 10:19 –

This book was written to focus on our hope as we
face the future. What has God promised will happen?
What things can we count on? The rest of the world
may see only dire situations ahead, but why can the
children of God have courage in going forward?
How are peace and joy and courage possible in the
times to come?

The Bible holds a wealth of prophecies about

what will happen on the world stage as its history spins away. I am neither a prophet nor a student of prophecy. I understand very little of the prophecies about what we call "the end times." But I am a student and pursuer of hope. There's so much we don't know and *can't* know—Scriptures even tell us we are not to know certain things. Yet there is so much we *can* know. So much of which we can be certain. That's what we want to contemplate together.

At the same time, we cannot ignore prophecies of the terrible times this world will see before all of God's plans are fulfilled. Throughout the Bible, we find references to times of great suffering and trouble that will come before the end of this world. Centuries before Jesus lived, prophets were given terrifying glimpses of what is still coming. When Jesus came to earth, He also gave us warnings. He described some of the things to come, explaining that these events were "the first of the birth pains, with more to come" (Mark 13:8). Like the pains of labor to bring about the birth of a child, this world is going to go through birth pains before the new world is born. Then, about sixty years after Jesus left the earth, the apostle John was given a revelation of what will happen at the end of earth's history. He saw not only the events on the earth but also the terrible conflicts in the spiritual realm.

As we look beyond today and consider the world moving toward the ultimate climax of God's plan, we can sense fear prowling around us, threatening to creep in and capture our minds and hearts.

What hope do we hold for living through such times? Until the day when Christ finally rules an earth filled with healing and peace and justice, what bridges of hope does God give us to get through the birth-pain times?

Let's go to the book of Daniel. It's an unusual book. It gives us some of the best-known Biblical stories we learned as children—Daniel in the lions' den and Shadrach, Meshach, and Abednego in the fiery furnace—and it also gives us prophecies about what is still to come. Because Daniel's visions are so puzzling and terrifying, I used to avoid that book. Something happened, though, during one of my yearly Bible read-throughs: Daniel turned out to be a book of hope!

Like jewels set against the darkness of what must happen, in Daniel we find messages of great hope for the children of God. And for the next few chapters, the prophet Daniel is going to speak to some of our questions.

As we read about the visions given to Daniel, we are not alone in our anxiety and unsettledness. Daniel himself was so upset by what he saw that he was physically ill.

But God sent an angel to explain things to Daniel. Oh, the kindness of God! And it was a kindness to us, too, because we now hear hope throughout the book.

The first jewel in the darkness is this word from the angel: "Don't be afraid. You are very precious to God. Peace! Be encouraged! Be strong!"

The angel repeats this three different times when he saw Daniel's confidence and courage waver. Since I've read the messages of Daniel, the Spirit has repeated it to me, too, when worry and fear knock at my door. *Don't be afraid. You are very precious to God.*

Oh, children of God! Do we need to know anything more than that?

MORE: Psalm 103:11; Psalm 117:2; John 14:27

 "THE FATHER LOVES YOU DEARLY"

But God is so rich in mercy, and he loved us so much.
- **EPHESIANS 2:4** -

I awoke to a sound I could not identify. A roar. Or a howling. Could it be the scream of a low-flying jet? But it was crashing through the woods behind our house. What is that?

A blizzard. Snow, wind, and ice left most of our county without power for four days. Many people were stranded in their homes, without heat or help. The local radio station put aside all programming and constantly streamed updates on emergency contacts, the progress of work to dig people out and restore services, and information on businesses that opened to help.

We had a three-month-old baby in need of formula, clean diapers, and heat. A fireplace gave little warmth, and we drained water from the water heater to mix formula. Sometime during that long wait for power to be restored, my brother-in-law and a friend tried to get to us through the drifted snow to drive us to town, to the warmth and safety of a house that did have power. From our living-room window high on the hill, we watched as the vehicle slowly pushed its way along the road below—but they were stopped a quarter-mile before our house and could go no farther.

That attempted mission failed. Yet it felt wonderful to know that someone had gone out into the cold, wind, and snow and risked their own safety to rescue us. Have you ever been rescued in a time of need? Can you recall your feelings of gratitude when someone cared enough to help you?

That feeling is nothing, though, compared to knowing that a man died to rescue me from an even more dangerous situation and bring me to safety.

Why would He? Why would God even bother to rescue me?

Why am I, a pinpoint in the universe, important to the Almighty Creator of it all?

Even more, why would He love me?

The answer is: He does.

I know, that doesn't answer the *why* question. But this is the fact of the heavenly realm that we need to soak up and hold on to: God loves us. And not because we are now His children. He loved us before He adopted us—while we were still on the enemy's side.

Now here is the danger, my friend: We might miss the awe of this fact.

Many of us have heard "God loves you" ever since we were little children. Even non-believers have heard it often. Can we set aside our familiarity with the words and hear them as though we've never heard them before?

And here's another hurdle: Among those whose mouths claim to believe this heavenly truth, there are many whose minds and hearts just can't believe it. The reality of it has never soaked into their bones.

The power of believing those three words is life-changing. So I pray the prayer of Ephesians 3:17-19 as I type this, asking that God will give us all a bigger experience of His love. As this passage says, His love is too great to understand fully. But verse 18 also asks for the "power to understand" the dimensions of God's love. Don't those two statements contradict themselves?

God's love for us is impossible to understand fully. But I do believe we begin to see the enormity of it as we experience it. Those words referring to measurements—height and depth, length and width—cannot be literal. No one measures love in that way. We understand it as a metaphor, a way of illustrating a truth.

In contrast, when Paul writes about the "measurements" of God's love, I believe he is not giving us a picture of the limits of God's love. Instead, Paul is trying to convey a sense of the immeasurable depth, height, width, and breadth of how much God treasures us. It's not something that is calculated and determined in any of our normal terms. It is only grasped through experience.

And our experience will never approach the outer limits of that love. I cannot say in what ways our heavenly Father is going to show you how much He loves you. A popular book these days talks about "love languages." Each of us has specific ways we show our love and specific ways we feel loved. I am certain of this, though—God will speak your love language! Because you are so precious to Him, He will make a point of speaking in a way you understand. I believe that.

(By the way, when I first read about "love

languages," I was struck by how all of the love languages are used in Scripture. Thus, different passages will speak to people based on their love language.)

My awe at the fact that God would care about me always deepens when I hear His words to me in Scripture. May I share some of my favorites with you?

> The Father himself loves you dearly. (John 16:27, Jesus speaking)

> And I say to you, "Don't be afraid. I am here to help you." (Isaiah 41:13, God speaking)

> We know how much God loves us, and we have put our trust in his love. (1 John 4:16)

> See how very much our Father loves us, for he calls us his children. (1 John 3:1)

> Unfailing love surrounds those who trust the LORD. (Psalm 32:10)

> The LORD watches over those... who rely on his unfailing love. (Psalm 33:18)

> To him who loves us and has freed us from our sins... (Revelation 1:5)

> Do not be afraid, for I have ransomed you. I have called you by name; you are mine. (Isaiah 43:1, God speaking)

WE'RE VERY PRECIOUS TO HIM

Give all your worries and cares to God, for
he cares about you. (1 Peter 5:7)

Start your own list of Scriptures that speak God's
love and care to you. Go to that list when you're
feeling unloved, inadequate, or alone.

It is not the *why* that we can know. We cannot
even know *how much,* since it goes beyond anything
we've ever experienced. But we can anchor our hope
to this: God has declared His love for us and acts on
it every day.

The experience of "feeling" God's love is not a
constant condition. Just as in human relationships,
emotions come and go, rise and fall. There are times
when we feel God's love, when it is as palpable as
arms embracing us. There are also times when we
do not feel loved. Yet our hope knows this: We are
very precious to God. He loves us. He has declared
we are His children, with all the rights and privileges
of heirs.

Let us look at what God's love has done and is
doing for us. And may His love pierce our hearts
anew as we *experience* it.

MORE: Romans 5:8; Romans 8:35-38; Ephesians 3:17-19

🍃 OUR GOD RESCUES 🍃

He rescues and saves his people; he performs miraculous
signs and wonders in the heavens and on earth.

— **DANIEL 6:27** —

Two of the best-known Old Testament stories are in the first half of the book of Daniel. They're often included in children's books of Bible stories. But as I read the book of Daniel in its entirety as an adult, I see details of these stories that I never knew as a child, details that fortify my hope in the God I trust.

My hope knows that God rescues and saves His people.

That hope is illustrated by the accounts of Daniel in the lions' den and of Shadrach, Meshach, and Abednego, Daniel's three friends who were thrown into the blazing furnace. These are stories of the incredible, miraculous rescue of God's faithful people. Dramatic and unforgettable stories.

As I read these stories yet one more time, I'm struck by several things.

First, the acknowledgment of God's mighty power to rescue His people comes from the mouths of pagan kings.

In both stories, the pagan kings are the ones who praise God when they see the miraculous rescue. They have seen the Almighty at work. After Daniel walked out of the lions' den without a scratch, King

Darius sent out a proclamation announcing his new belief in Daniel's saving God. When the three friends were brought out of the furnace without one hair sizzled or a whiff of smoke on their clothes, Nebuchadnezzar exclaimed, "There is no other god who can rescue like this!"

No, King Neb, there is no other god like ours.

Sisters and brothers, children of the Most High God—other gods today might look powerful and might appear to offer us salvation. But none treasure us as our God does, and none can rescue us like our Rescuer can.

You may have had a rescue in your life as miraculous as Daniel being saved from the lions. God is still doing such miracles today. But for every one of us, He is also doing "everyday" miracles. Maybe today He held your tongue when you wanted to spew bitter words. Maybe you were wavering in the face of a strong temptation, and the Spirit rescued you. Maybe He calmed a storm and led you beside still waters. Maybe He took an impossibly frantic schedule and smoothed the way for you or strengthened you in a way that amazed you. Maybe His protection caused you to hesitate for a moment before making a turn—so that the car running a red light did not hit you. Maybe your discouragement or depression was lifted by a conversation with a friend. Maybe the Spirit gave you peace and calmness as you listened to the doctor talk about treatment. Maybe when you sat down for devotions this morning and your soul cried out to God, He led you to the very words of Scripture you needed to hear. Have you seen God's wonderful rescues on a daily basis?

We are very precious to Him. He is here, right here with us, walking through every fire with us, just as He did with the men in the furnace. Big and little rescues and saves—He excels at them all.

I was with a friend during a time of family crisis. Normally strong and full of faith, she came under a tremendous attack of fear. She was in tears; I didn't know what to say or do for her, but she asked me to pray. My prayer was for her peace. Not a solution to the problem right then. Just calmness. Before the hour was up, she received a telephone call from someone neither of us would have ever expected to call. I had not even thought to ask God for this! And that call put her mind at ease. Peace. The storm quieted. A rescue from the powerful enemy of fear. It was far better than anything I could have imagined!

Expect His rescue, and then watch for it. God knows how to rescue His treasured children. You can count on that as you head down the road toward tomorrow.

Daniel's three friends, who refused to bow down to anyone but God, stood firm with a strength I want. "Our God is able to save us from anything," they said to the king, "but even if he chooses not to save us from this fire, we will never serve anyone but Him."

May our faith in our God and in what He does for His people be this unwavering. Even if we have to walk into the fire—or we're thrown into it. May we hold on to our hope and never serve anyone but Him.

MORE: *Psalm 37:39-40; Psalm 68:20; Psalm 145:19*

 **FIRST AND FINAL RESCUES**

Jesus gave his life... to rescue us.
- GALATIANS 1:4 -

From beginning to end, the Bible is the narrative of God's rescue of His creation. He did not turn His back on the world, or burn it up as a hopeless cause. His plan was and is and will always be rescue.

John 3:16 is the most oft-quoted verse about God's rescue plan. That plan was in place even before the angel assigned to duty at the gate of Eden had taken up his flaming sword. The entirety of the Bible traces God's plan in action.

So where are we in this history of God's rescue plan? And how does it give us courage as we face tomorrow?

We have to backtrack a bit and go back to our own rescue. Scripture says that Jesus gave His life to rescue us. Rescue us from what? I confess that I first believed in Jesus only because I wanted Him to save me from hell. I sat in an evangelistic meeting and listened to the preacher declaring that only the pure in heart would see God—and I knew I was not pure in heart. I was doomed to eternal punishment. I asked Jesus to save me from that.

But along the way, in the many years since, I've discovered that His rescue is so much more! From what has Jesus rescued you? Here are some Scriptures that will start our list. I'd like to write more about all of them because these are all so important to me. But read them, think about your own rescue, and tell Him how grateful you are.

- From this evil world. (Galatians 1:4)

- From the curse pronounced on me because of my wrongdoing. He took the curse on Himself! (Galatians 3:13)

- From the kingdom of darkness. And He transferred us to His kingdom of light. Reminds me of being "transplanted to God's courts." (Colossians 1:13)

- From the terrors of the coming judgment. (1 Thessalonians 1:10)

- From empty lives. (1 Peter 1:18)

- From every kind of sin. (Titus 2:14)

- From my sinful nature—no one else
  could! (Romans 6:14; 8:12)

- From the fear of death. (Hebrews 2:14, 15)

All right, so I couldn't resist adding a few comments on my own.

I'm going to list Psalm 107 in the MORE section below. Take time to read the entire chapter if you did not read it earlier. It recounts ways God rescues those who call to Him for help. My story is there. I have a feeling you also will recognize yourself in one of the accounts.

And then, we look forward to God's final, complete rescue of His people.

In the last half of his book, Daniel recorded his visions of the future. I can't untangle exactly what all of these prophecies foresee. Some of the events seem to have already happened in Israel's history. Yet the angel messenger tells Daniel at one point, "What you are seeing pertains to the very end of time" (Daniel 8:19). Daniel is given a numbering of days—but remember, we are also told that "days" means a very different thing to God than the literal meaning we give it. I don't even try to sort it all out.

But here's a promise of hope: Michael, the angel messenger, spoke of a terrible time of great anguish, greater than at any other time in the world's history. "But at that time, every one of your people whose name is written in the book will be rescued" (Daniel 12:1). Whether already dead or still alive, God's people will be rescued in the end.

And this is the detail that matters most to me: God's final, full rescue of His people.

Let me amend that statement, because that's not a "detail." That is the entire story!

That's the reason our hope goes forward in great expectation. We are very precious to God. We can depend on Him to save His people. Today, tomorrow, and at the very end of time.

Peace! Be encouraged! Be strong!

MORE: Psalm 107; Psalm 144:7; 1 Timothy 2:6; 2 Peter 2:9

 **GOD'S CHOICE**

For God chose to save us through our Lord Jesus Christ, not to pour out his anger on us.
- **1 THESSALONIANS 5:9** -

In the previous meditation, I suggested you read a list of the many ways Jesus has rescued you and express your gratitude to Him. But maybe that list did not fill you with gratitude. Perhaps you instead felt a despair that you have not experienced all of that. Or perhaps the thought of the end of this world fills you with fear instead of expectation—because you know you are not ready for that day to come.

Tell God you want peace with Him. The Good News is that you can have it—no matter who or what you've been.

> This is the message of Good News... that there is peace with God through Jesus Christ, who is Lord of all. (Acts 10:36)

> Everyone who believes in him is declared right with God. (Acts 13:39)

God has made the choice to offer this peace to you. You have the choice of taking His gift or refusing it.

But know that He is waiting and wants to rescue you. He wants to plant you in a place where you will flourish and to supply what you need. He wants you to understand the truth and be set free from lies. He wants to live with you and be your God. He wants to give you peace, courage, and strength because you are very precious to Him.

Yes, you *are* very precious to Him, even if you do not yet belong to Christ. God sent His Son on a rescue mission. He came to cancel the record of charges against us. He came to make our peace with God.

There will be an end to time. But now, at this moment, God is still choosing to show His mercy to anyone who comes to Him.

God made another choice that also boggles my mind. We can ask *why?* But God simply tells us He does this because He wants to:

> God decided in advance to adopt us into his own family by bringing us to himself through Jesus Christ. This is what he wanted to do, and it gave him great pleasure. (Ephesians 1:5)

From enemy to heir. God loved me even while I was ignoring Him and doing things my own way. Have you had a wayward, rebellious child? Have you found it difficult to love them? Know that God loves the wayward and rebellious. Or maybe your love for that rebellious child held strong through all the storms; know that God's love is even stronger.

And so God's love put a plan in place to bring rebels back into His family and give them all the rights and blessings of a son or daughter. That plan was Jesus Christ, and everybody who believes and receives Him is given "the right to become children of God" (John 1:12).

Ephesians 3:6 speaks of the "riches inherited by God's children." As we noted before, these riches are something we can live on *now*. We don't have to wait for our inheritance, although the full inheritance will come sometime in the future. But a bounty is ours for today, and tomorrow, and the day after that, and the day after that.

I'm beginning to see—only beginning, mind you— how little we understand how privileged we are and how we fail to grasp the bounty of the inheritance. But the promises are there, in God's Word to us. *He tells us what we can have as His children.* That's what the Hope Knows books are all about—learning to live as children of God, living out our inheritance.

This is what God has chosen to do for us. Has there ever been a greater gift? Don't try to figure out the *why*. Instead, concentrate on how amazing this is. Does it change how you view yourself? You are not just a pinpoint in the universe, but someone precious to God.

MORE: *Ezekiel 33:11; John 3:17; Galatians 3:29; Titus 3:4, 5; 2 Peter 3:9*

〜 HE LISTENS 〜

So let us come boldly to the throne of our gracious God.
There we will receive his mercy, and we will find grace to
help us when we need it the most.

- HEBREWS 4:16 -

Have you had the experience of talking to someone about an issue that's very important to you, a burden that is heavy on your heart, or perhaps an incident that gave you great joy—and you suddenly noticed that the other person wasn't at all interested? Few people can pretend real interest if they are bored.

If you have gathered by now that much of what this chapter covers amazes me—you're right. I'm amazed that God cares about me. That He says I am His daughter, with His blessings and resources available to me. That He has canceled and forgotten my previous record. And here is something more: He hears my prayers, and He cares about everything, from the smallest wisp of worry to the most monstrous mountains in my life. He listens, and He cares.

The Maker of the universe listens to all my prayers with a heart of love. The foolish prayers. The heartbroken prayers. The joyous prayers. The adoring prayers. The desperate prayers. The contrite and ashamed prayers. The confused prayers. He listens to it all. He never gets bored and turns away.

Tell me, do you have anyone in your life who cares this much about you?

What do you talk to God about?

Luke 12:6, 7 gives us the words of Jesus, telling us that God doesn't forget about one little sparrow, and His children are so much more loved and cared for than sparrows that He even keeps track of each hair on my head. He must care about the smallest details of my life—things to which I don't even pay attention.

Yes, I pray about "little" things. I've asked Him to remind me where I put something I've temporarily lost, or I've asked for the energy to get through a meeting, or I've thanked Him for a beautiful morning sky. Small things in my day. I believe Psalm 37:23: "He delights in every detail of [our] lives."

And we must remember that this God who cares so much about our lives is the great, all-powerful Maker who created this universe. He can also do the impossible! We can ask great things of Him, too.

At one point, Daniel stood trembling before the angel messenger. Trembling. This was a man who stood fearlessly in front of pagan kings and gave them news they did not want to hear. He stood firm in his worship of God, refusing to buckle at the threat of being thrown to the lions. Yet the appearance of the messenger from God shook him so much that he fainted. A hand helped him to his hands and knees, and the man said,

Don't be afraid, Daniel. Since the first day you began to pray for understanding and to humble yourself before your God, your request has been heard in heaven. I have come in answer to your prayer. (Daniel 10:12)

Note two things here: One, that a heavenly messenger comes as an answer to prayer. This would leave many of us shaken! And yet, God does that for us, His children. We may not see a messenger in the image we have of angels or heavenly beings, but when we come to God seeking understanding and with a humble heart, He does send us answers and messengers. Sometimes, His message to us might come through another person or circumstances. Sometimes it is through His Word. Sometimes it is through the miraculous connection we have to Him—His Holy Spirit within.

Father, open our eyes and ears to the messengers you send.

The other thing that strikes me is that from the first day Daniel prayed, his request was heard. At another place in Daniel, the messenger said, "the moment you began praying, a command was given" (Daniel 9:23).

Daniel was praying for his people, a nation in despair, a people who had wandered far from God. Daniel's prayer is passionate and agonizing. (Read it in Daniel 9:1-19.)

We might be tempted to say that God responded to Daniel immediately because of Daniel's devotion to God and that powerful prayer. Does God respond in the same way to our prayers? Does He care that much about us?

In Hebrews, we find the door open for us, too. Jesus' death ripped apart the barrier between God and us. We can go directly to Him with the outpouring of our own hearts. What will His response be? Kindness and help. (See the opening verse.)

It is not only calls for help that are heard by God.

- He hears our prayers for others. (1 Timothy 2:1)

- He delights in hearing our thanks for what He has done and our praise and worship of who He is. (Hebrews 12:28, 13:15)

- When our penitent heart comes before Him, He will always respond to our words of confession and repentance. (Isaiah 55:7, Psalm 51:1-17)

As we live out whatever is coming in the future, our hope knows that our God will hear and respond to our prayers. Our prayers do matter!

MORE: Psalm 27:8; Psalm 34:17, 18; Psalm 116:2; Ephesians 6:18

❧ "DON'T BE AFRAID" ❧

Give all your worries and cares to God, for he cares about you.

- 1 PETER 5:7 -

I know you've heard the following words many times, but read them today and hear Jesus say them to *you.*

Oh, and one other thing. I also know this is a difficult passage for most of us. We haven't figured out exactly how to apply it to our lives. It goes against everything this world teaches and preaches. It's in direct contradiction to dictates like, Be practical! Be strong and self-sufficient! You must plan for the future! Build your security! Be responsible! The world around us would roll their eyes at what Jesus is saying. They'd be stern, and admonish: This is foolishness. Don't be absurd. Be realistic.

But Jesus is telling us about a reality of the Kingdom of Heaven. Are we going to believe Him?

And if God cares so wonderfully for flowers that are here today and thrown into the fire tomorrow, he will certainly care for you. Why do you have so little faith? And don't be concerned about what to eat and what to drink. Don't worry about such things. Those things dominate the thoughts of unbelievers all over the world, but your Father already knows your needs. Seek the Kingdom of God above all else, and he will give you everything you need. So don't be afraid, little flock. For it gives your Father great happiness to give you the Kingdom. (Luke 12:28-32)

So much in these few paragraphs warms my heart! I cannot know which of these words the Spirit used to speak to you today, but here are some that have anchored my hope.

God knows everything I need. He is keeping watch! Psalm 121 is a short psalm of just eight verses, yet five times the declaration is made that God watches over me. He created me. He knows what I need—even when I sometimes don't know myself and don't know what to ask for. He knows. And He keeps an eye on me.

He will *certainly* care for me. Jesus says there is no doubt. The Old Testament gives us accounts of God watching over His people, caring for their needs, protecting them. Jesus tells us He is the Great Shepherd, our champion, the one who will watch over us, the one who would even die for us. Certainly He'll care for me. Don't doubt it!

"Don't worry about such things..." Did it occur to you that the "such things" Jesus mentioned are what we would call absolute necessities? Food and drink, essential to life. But Jesus said they'll be provided. Don't worry.

The Father is delighted to give us His Kingdom! Now, I don't know what all that will entail—but it's my inheritance, from the Father who loves me. I do know He says I can have and use some of my inheritance now. That leaves me a little breathless with anticipation and desire to know more.

"Don't be afraid, little flock." To me, these are the most comforting words of all. Can you hear the tenderness in Jesus' voice as He says this to anxious disciples?

Every time I read this passage, I have to ask the Spirit to show me more of how I can apply this to my life—how to let go, trust, and not worry. We are anxious. We do worry about tomorrow. But my King tells me, "Don't be afraid. I'm the Great Shepherd. I will take care of you."

I know this is a difficult teaching. We're all at different stages in learning how to let go of our need to control our lives and, instead, grab the confident promise that God has things under control and we don't need to worry.

The Father is pleased to give us His Kingdom. *The Kingdom!* And He knows how many hairs fell from your head this morning. We are, indeed, in a place of great privilege, and we can go confidently and joyfully into tomorrow because God will take care of His treasured children.

My cup overflows.

MORE: Psalm 23; Psalm 55:22; Matthew 6:25-34

☙ GOD IS FOR US ❧

For since the world began, no ear has heard and no eye has seen a God like you, who works for those who wait for him!

— ISAIAH 64:4 —

What greater hope can we have as we face the future than to know that we are very precious to God, so precious that He has adopted us as His children?

If God is for us, as Paul phrased it in Romans 8:31, how can we not feel courage, peace, and strength as we face whatever we'll meet on the road tomorrow? In the same chapter, Paul goes through quite a list of disasters and powers of darkness that might test us— but nothing can cut us off from God's love.

If you've started to create your own list of Scriptures that give you the assurance you are precious to God, may I suggest adding this: "The eternal God is your refuge, and his everlasting arms are under you" (Deuteronomy 33:27). That may be from one of the first books in the Bible, but we are talking about the *eternal* God. What He was then, He is now, and He always will be. Everlasting arms holding you—dwell in that refuge.

And then there is the question of your inheritance. If you received word that a large inheritance awaited you, wouldn't you immediately ask exactly what this inheritance was? I hope you're asking that now. I hope that all of us are inspired to find out more of what

God has for us even while we are still here on earth. Such knowledge will make us stronger and more courageous as we face the future. And the more we make use of our inheritance, the more we will see our God at work for His children. My hope knows and lives on that.

So, while my purpose in writing is to help and encourage hope in both you and me, my prayer is that it also inspires you to go to God's Word. That's where you'll find the best help and hope. The Spirit will show you promises you need, promises you can depend on. Read the Scriptures—they are God's words to you. He wants you to know what He will do for His children.

God works for those who put their hope and trust in Him. And even when our faith falters, He always answers the prayer of *Help my unbelief!*

Our God is living with His people, traveling the road with them as He guides them home. Know Him, and know who you are to Him.

MORE: Isaiah 43:1-5; Romans 8:28; 1 John 4:16

PRAYER FOR TIMES OF DOUBT:

Reassure me of your promise.

– **PSALM 119:38** –

OUR GOD RULES
AND HAS A PLAN

⌬ IN THE HAND OF THE FIRST ⌬
AND THE LAST

He will feed his flock like a shepherd. He will carry the
lambs in his arms, holding them close to his heart. He will
gently lead the mother sheep with their young.

– ISAIAH 40:11 –

"It was a good thing at one time. It began because there was a need for it." He shook his head regretfully. "But look at it now. Too big. Too strong. Too corrupt. Hurting us more than helping us."

I won't tell you what we were talking about, but you might guess. And many different guesses might be correct—that assessment could fit any one of multiple ideas and entities. Look around at our world. There's a long list of projects that we humans have begun for good reasons but that have been poisoned and twisted when the sinful nature got involved. Doesn't that seem to be the history of most of our initiatives? Everything big or small, from government and insurance companies to, yes, even our church organizations and our celebration of Christmas.

I usually begin with the best of intentions, too. But things don't always turn out so well. My old sinful nature sneaks in, and intentions and actions go off on the wrong track. What happens across the entire face of the earth also happens in the small sphere I inhabit—and in my internal world.

Whether we're talking about personal history or world history, if everything begins and ends with us, our track record does not bode well for the future.

Ah, but my hope knows this: Our future does not begin and end with us.

> When I saw him, I fell at his feet as if I were dead. But he laid his right hand on me and said, "Don't be afraid! I am the First and the Last. I am the living one. I died, but look—I am alive forever and ever! And I hold the keys of death and the grave." (Revelation 1:17, 18)

John is describing his encounter with Jesus—many years after Jesus had left the earth. John was absolutely overcome with awe and humility at Jesus' glorious presence, so heavenly and powerful. And the Lord's first words to John? "Don't be afraid."

Those words and the seven that follow speak peace to my soul. They tell me that our God holds this world in His hands. He created this world. He has a plan for it. Everything begins and ends with Him. And look at the tenderness in the opening verse from Isaiah. The Almighty First and Last is a Shepherd who so lovingly cares for His flock.

He holds my life in His hands. He gave me a new, eternal life. He began it—and He has great plans for it. The beginning and the end and everything in between are in His hands.

And He tells me not to be afraid.

Billy Graham has been quoted as saying that since he read the last page of the Bible, he knew everything would turn out all right. For me, reading the entire Bible through chronologically (it's not as difficult as you might think), has been a huge taste of the power of the age to come—we read about God's hand in the past, His dealings with us in the present, and His assurance to His children concerning the future.

God says He has a plan for the world He began, and He is always working toward the end He intends to bring about. And even though my life is just a breath in the history of this world, He is doing the same for me in my personal history and in the purposes for which He created me. Imagine that!

He gave me my beginning. He holds me now. He knows my end—what and where I will be when His plans come to completion.

And He tells me not to be afraid!

MORE: Psalm 138:8; Proverbs 19:21; Isaiah 41:13

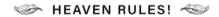 **HEAVEN RULES!**

His rule is everlasting, and his kingdom is eternal.
- DANIEL 4:34 -

The book of Daniel trumpets another hope we can hold on to through the birth-pain times. This truth is illustrated in the accounts of two kings.

King Nebuchadnezzar and his successor, Belshazzar, came face to face with this reality. One king came to the truth in time to save himself and his kingdom. The other refused to acknowledge it and lost both his kingdom and his life.

This is the truth: the Most High rules forever!

Nebuchadnezzar was a rich, powerful king, controlling most of his known world. It was his empire that had smashed Judah and moved Daniel and many other Jews to Babylon as captives. Nebuchadnezzar had conquered every nation he went against. In time, he became proud and arrogant as he surveyed all he had accomplished and built. He even had a statue of himself erected and ordered people to worship there.

At this point, God let him know: You must learn that "the Most High rules over the kingdoms of the world, and gives them to anyone he chooses." (See Daniel 4.)

Through a dream, God warned the king that he would lose his sanity for a period of time. But all was not lost. Nebuchadnezzar could still regain his kingdom, "when you have learned that heaven rules."

And that is what happened. This arrogant, idolatrous ruler learned. We don't know the details of how his sanity was restored and how he came to worship God, but chapter 4 of Daniel records the king's own words after he regained his sanity and his throne. He announced his new allegiance to and worship of the Most High King.

> I want you all to know about the miraculous signs and wonders the Most High God has performed for me. How great are his signs, how powerful his wonders! His kingdom will last forever, his rule through all generations. (Daniel 4:2, 3)

These words of worship came from the pagan

king! Chapter 4 is the king's own telling of his story, in a report sent to every part of his empire. The most powerful king in the world at that time ended his message by honoring "the one who lives forever. His rule is everlasting and his kingdom is eternal... He does as he pleases... no one can stop him." Nebuchadnezzar had learned that there was no other God, and heaven rules.

His successor, Belshazzar, knew everything that had happened to Nebuchadnezzar, yet he defied God. He, too, was rich, powerful, and proud. Daniel had a message from God for this king also: "You have not honored the God who gives you the breath of life and controls your destiny" (Daniel 5:23). And so God took the kingdom from Belshazzar. That very night, the king was assassinated.

Satan is at war with God, and this earth is a weary, bloody battlefield. We must journey through the battlefield for a time, but God still holds supreme dominion. The birth pains tell us a new world is coming, where God's plans will win out. We belong to the one kingdom that will endure forever.

Even in what seems to be the worst of times, our hope can live on these words: Heaven rules! He alone is God. There is no other—never has been, never will be.

MORE: *Deuteronomy 4:35; Psalm 103:19; Isaiah 43:10; Acts 17:24-26*

 A PLAN FOR THE WHOLE EARTH

"Everything under heaven is mine."

\- JOB 41:11 -

"I have a plan for the whole earth."

\- ISAIAH 14:26 -

Have we forgotten?

Have we forgotten that all of creation belongs to the Lord? He made it. He claims it.

Yes, this world has been invaded by God's enemy. Both the natural world and humankind are suffering under bondage to the death and decay brought by Satan. But all of creation still belongs to God, and God has a plan for it.

Our vision is far too restricted if we think the story is only that God created the world and its people and then humanity made a choice that derailed God's intentions and so God gave us yet one more chance to be in right relationship with Him. That is all true, but when we look at Scriptures more closely, we see that God's plan reaches far beyond that limited outline. His plan is for a new creation, for an eternal kingdom of peace and justice, and for the healing of all that has gone wrong.

God assures us that He has plans for the natural world, plans for those He loves, and plans for those who refuse to believe, who resist and rebel against Him. Yes, He also has plans for Satan and the spiritual forces he leads.

Isn't this comforting? The King we follow is not at the mercy of any other force in the universe. He *is* The Force. He is going to accomplish His purposes. He is working, hour by hour, and His plan is unfolding. Nothing will stop Him.

This is the hope. Our faith moves forward on that bridge of hope. We live in a world of trouble, pain, and death, an imperfect, unsatisfying, disappointing world. But in the midst of all that has gone wrong with this world—and within ourselves!—we believe our God when He says there is a plan, and it will all happen according to His purpose. And so we keep moving forward with our eyes on Him.

The second of our opening verses—God's declaration that He has plans for the whole world—is embedded in a prophecy about judgment on a number of pagan countries. But this is an overarching statement that goes beyond specific prophecies for certain countries. He has plans for the whole world. He is not a detached, distant God who has left this earth to create its own destiny.

I find peace in knowing that God governs the future—the same God to whom we are precious, the God who walks with us, and the God who says to us, "Don't be afraid."

MORE: *Psalm 24:1; Psalm 33:11, 12; Psalm 89:11; Isaiah 46:10*

A PLAN FOR HIS CHILDREN

O LORD my God, you have performed many wonders for us.
Your plans for us are too numerous to list.

- **PSALM 40:5** -

The second line of our opening verse says God's plans for us are too numerous to list. It's no wonder, then, that I don't even know where to start this short meditation on God's plans for His children.

Our hope knows this: God has plans for us.

Let's stop there for a moment and let the comfort of that surround us.

God has plans for us. We are His treasured children, and our future is in His hands.

How that changes the look of tomorrow!

One way God communicates His plans to us is through His promises. For example, we have His promise that He is living here with us and will guide us throughout all of life. That's part of His plan for His children—to be right here with us, involved in our lives, being our God.

In His Word, God tells us a great deal about His plans for His children. And, because the psalmist was right and it's too enormous a subject to tackle in a page or two, I only want to point out some interesting facts God gives us concerning these plans.

> For God saved us... not because we deserved
> it, but because that was his plan from before
> the beginning of time. (2 Timothy 1:9)

God planned our rescue before the beginning of time. This is difficult for us to grasp because we are so enmeshed in the structure of time. The one thing we can hold on to, though, is that God's plan has always been rescue—He did not abandon His creation, but planned a rescue.

> And now he has made all of this plain to us by
> the appearing of Christ Jesus, our Savior. He
> broke the power of death and illuminated the
> way to life and immortality. (2 Timothy 1:10)

Peter also wrote of Jesus' role in the rescue. He wrote that before the world began, Jesus was chosen as the ransom for us. And look what He accomplished. He broke the power of death and showed the way to life and immortality. For people who were trapped by the certainty of death—that's rescue! And don't miss this: He shows us the way to life. Not just immortal life, but life here and now. Don't we all want life now? It's in the plan.

> He made [His plan] for our ultimate glory
> before the world began. (1 Corinthians 2:7)

There's the phrase again: "before the world began." But now we also have the other end of our history—our ultimate glory. Suddenly, we break the limits of time. God's plan to rescue His children began before time, and the range of His plan goes on forever—after the end of time. You are not an accident, a chance happening, a nothing, floating along with no purpose or destiny. You are not insignificant, a speck in the universe who is here today and, *poof,* gone tomorrow. Your heavenly Father has plans for you long after world history ends. You are His child, precious to Him.

God planned for you to bear the same glory He does. Humans were created in God's image. That was lost, but God's plan is to restore the image of Himself in you. Hebrews 1:3 says that Christ "radiates God's own glory and expresses the very character of God." And the Spirit of Christ is living in each of His children and changing them to be like Him!

So God has already put the plan into motion. He's begun this process in your life, here and now. He is not waiting until "someday" to suddenly transform you into a glorious being. This part of your eternal life has already begun.

This is humbling. God wants to do that in me? Yes, His plan for His children is that they *share* His glory. In John 17:22, Jesus said He gave His disciples the same glory that God gave Him. And that was not only for His small circle of disciples in that day. Colossians 1:27 tells us that Christ now lives in us and gives us "assurance of sharing his glory." In 2 Corinthians 3:18, that the Spirit is making us more and more like Christ every day, as we are "changed into his glorious image." And Romans 8:23 says that this work of the Spirit within us is a "foretaste of future glory." It's happening now!

This is God's plan for you, child of God. And if you still have lingering doubts about your worth, your destiny, or God's plan for you, read Hebrews 2:10, 11 and try to absorb those surprising words: God has chosen to bring many children into glory, and Jesus is not ashamed to call you His sister or brother!

> No eye has seen, no ear has heard, and no mind has imagined what God has prepared for those who love him. (1 Corinthians 2:9)

We can't imagine it. The plan for our glory is almost beyond our comprehension. And there is so much more. He has plans that He works out on a daily basis: His plan to guide you. To give you good gifts. To encourage you. To bring hope to your life. To provide for you. To strengthen you. To revive you when you lie in the dust. To make Himself known to you. To give you a new heart and a new life. Yes, even to give you a new identity, purpose, and mission in life.

Ecclesiastes 3:11 tells us that God "has planted eternity in the human heart, but even so, people cannot see the whole scope of God's work from beginning to end."

We can't comprehend it all. But the wonderful tastes we are given of the power of God's plan will give us courage, peace, and joy as we go forward into tomorrow.

MORE: *2 Corinthians 3:18; 1 Thessalonians 2:12; 2 Peter 1:3, 4*

THE KING WE FOLLOW

Now he is far above any ruler or authority or power or leader or anything else—not only in this world, but also in the world to come.

- EPHESIANS 1:21 -

God owns His creation. He has plans for all of it—including you and me. We are in the hands of the First and the Last, who tells us not to be afraid. Let's fix our thoughts, for a few minutes, on our Champion, the one who lived on the earth as a human being like us and is now alive and leading us along the path of God's plans.

We have put our trust in the one who holds highest honors in the heavens. "All the angels and authorities and powers accept his authority" (1 Peter 3:22). His assurance to us that He has overcome all the powers in the world is not an empty promise. Colossians 2:15 says that He disarmed all other spiritual powers, shaming them in a public spectacle by what He did on the cross. What human eyes saw that day was the execution of a man who was seen as too radical. He was just another troublemaker put to death by the authorities. However, in unseen, spiritual realms that day, a battle was raging—its outcome would prove the rule and authority of our King.

He won.

He was a human like us. As you imagine these scenes, think of a man. Jesus was not God play-acting as a human. He was a man with all the emotions that we have—including anxiety and fear. In the Garden of Gethsemane, the night before his arrest, he experienced such anxiety that his sweat contained blood. This is a rare condition that occurs when a person is under extreme stress or fear. (The medical term is hematidrosis.) And can you imagine his anguish as he died? He had devoted his life to what he knew was God's plan and endured ridicule, criticism, and rejection while he was teaching. He was tortured before his execution. But the worst blow of all came at the very last moment of his life. Then, he believed God had abandoned him.

He had given up all the things most people want in life—family, home, and security—and suffered all this for his God and God's plan. And then God turned away when Jesus needed Him the most.

He would gladly have taken another path if he could have. But his prayer was that God's will would be done—and God's plan required this of Jesus so that the break between God and His creation could be repaired.

About seven hundred years before Jesus was born, a prophecy told us something that is a great comfort for me today. Isaiah delivered messages from God about the coming Messiah: He would be crushed, and it would appear that His life achieved nothing. But "the LORD's good plan will prosper in his hands" (Isaiah 53:10).

Jesus, seeming to lose everything as he died, won everything. And God's plan took giant strides forward.

Find a time when you can clear your mind of all else. Sit down and ask God to give you a glimpse of His great plan, and then read Isaiah 53.

As a result of his submission to God's plan, Jesus the Rescuer now holds all authority in the heavens and on earth, in this history and in the future world to come.

Your hope can know, child of God, that you belong to this Jesus, who is supreme. He holds your future and God's plans for you in His hands. And the plan, under His guidance, will prosper!

MORE: *Matthew 28:18; Hebrews 2:10; Hebrews 12:2*

HE WILL DO IT

I am God. There is none like me. I am the only one who can tell you about the future. And everything I plan will come to pass, for I can accomplish all my purposes. I have said what I will do, and I will do it.

- ISAIAH 46:9-11 AP -

Try to imagine what it would be like.

A foreign power invades your town. Many of the town's leaders, professional people, intellectuals, and skilled workers are pulled out of their homes and shipped off to another country to live under that foreign ruler. And, let's just say, you are among those who are now a long, long way from home, living in a strange culture and an environment hostile to your beliefs and customs. You grieve for your home, your town, your neighbors, friends, and family. Your life as you have always known it has been destroyed.

Then a letter comes from a prophet back home. He has a message from God for you. Part of that message is "I have plans for you. Plans for good and a future. Hopeful plans. I will do all the things I have promised you" (Jeremiah 29:11 AP).

That's a word of hope. But then there was this additional word: "You'll be there for seventy years, and then I promise to bring you back home."

Oh. Seventy years.

God has given us all this message in His Word: *I have good plans for you.* Our hope knows His promises and anchors to them. We trust God to deliver on what He has promised.

But I wonder how we might feel and what we would think if, along with the message of good plans, we were told, "But your current situation is going to go on for seventy years. *Then* I'll do what I promised you."

We are impatient people these days. That's one reason why patience comes only as a fruit of the Spirit living in us. Patience is not a natural reaction— especially when we're dealing with unpleasant circumstances.

Would we begin to wonder if God really will be true to His word?

He might have wonderful plans for us, but can we trust Him to stick to the plan?

The opening verses are a summary of dozens (maybe hundreds) of places in God's Word where He says, "I will do everything I've promised. It will happen. I will do it!" God says this in the prophecies of the future, and He says it when He promises us He is working today.

The apostle Paul wrote with great confidence:

And I am certain that God, who began the good work within you, will continue his work until it is finally finished on the day when Christ Jesus returns. (Philippians 1:6)

I know the one in whom I trust, and I am sure that he is able to guard what I have entrusted to him until the day of his return. (2 Timothy 1:12)

Knowing nurtures trust. Read God's Word to get to know Him. The God you find there is the one who lives with you today and says, "I do not change" (Malachi 3:6). Read His Word so that you also know what He has planned and promised. The better you know Him, the stronger will be your trust, the greater will be your peace, and the more courageous will be your walk along the road tomorrow.

MORE: Deuteronomy 7:9; Psalm 138:8; 1 Thessalonians 5:24

CAPTIVATED ANGELS

But Jesus replied, "My Father is always working, and so am I."
- JOHN 5:17 -

In 1 Peter chapter 1, the apostle gave us a glimpse into heavenly realms that I find fascinating. It's one short line of Scripture, but tuck it away in your head and heart. Bring it out and dwell on it when the day is hard, or when your path ahead looks too crooked and rocky to continue, or when you are just plain bored with the ordinary and common things of life.

Before we look at that Scripture, let's set the stage.

Peter the apostle is writing to God's people scattered in other countries. (That would be us, too, brothers and sisters.) They're under fire for following Christ. They need encouragement. (That would also be us. We are always targeted by the enemy.)

Peter reminds them (and us) of God's great mercy. His undeserved kindness has given us this new life as children of God. There's an inheritance we can claim, both now and in the future. We can be truly glad, he writes, because there is great joy ahead. Be joyful even through testing and trials. Your faith will turn into something more precious than gold. Trusting Jesus through everything will be the rescue of your soul.

Peter explained that the prophets had talked about this long ago, even though they didn't understand how or when it was all going to come about. But now, it is happening! This is the plan God made even before the world began. And God is keeping His promises.

Now, here's the verse to ponder: Peter wrote, "It is all so wonderful that even the angels are eagerly watching these things happen" (1 Peter 1:12).

And that encouragement is for us today, too. As Jesus said, He and the Father are always working. Every day, God is unfolding His promises and plans for us.

He has not forgotten or changed His mind. He is not asleep. He is not uncaring, detached, or dead. He's working in the world today. He is working in the lives of His children. He is calling people back to Him. His plans for His creation are moving forward, and He's keeping His promises.

Need a taste of the power of the age that is coming? Then think about the angels—captivated by the way God is at work, unfolding His wonderful plans.

MORE: Psalm 108:1; Psalm 145:13; Romans 4:20-22

PRAYER IN TIMES OF TEARS:

O God, give me comfort in my suffering.

Renew my life by your promises.

– **PSALM 119:50 AP** –

EXPECTATION OF OUR TEARS

 CRUSHED

But it was the LORD's good plan to crush
him and cause him grief.

- ISAIAH 53:10 -

Deepest grief. Sorrows. Beaten. Weighed down. Punished. Whipped. Crushed.

Do any of those words bring immediate tears because you are currently *there?*

And that opening verse—how can a plan to crush someone and cause him grief be a good plan? And why would a plan for such suffering come from the Lord?

That's the question we are most prone to ask when we are in the midst of suffering or grief: Why?

The verse from Isaiah is referring to the Messiah, the one who would come to rescue His people. And Scripture tells us that if we count ourselves as belonging to Jesus, then we, too, can expect that suffering and tears will be part of our journey. We are of one kingdom, this world is of another, and the powers of this world line up in active opposition to citizens of Christ's kingdom.

The title of this chapter is "Expectation of Our Tears." The words have a double meaning. One, as we look toward the future, we can expect tears. We know that pain and grief are waiting along the path of every human on this earth. God doesn't bubble wrap His children; we'll suffer all the loss, conflict, and trouble common to humanity. Yet, our hope sees promise in suffering—even though we see it through our tears.

And that is the second meaning of this chapter title. We live in great expectation, even when we are weighed down, bewildered, and besieged. Even then, God has given us bridges of hope to carry us across those chasms.

It feels almost disrespectful to have one short chapter on suffering. Trials and tears cut deeply and shred lives. We cannot treat this subject lightly. But let me say, first of all, that all of these short chapters are on subjects carrying so much promise we will never come to the end of discovering all the hope God gives us. That's why there are MORE Scriptures for each meditation so that you can dig deeper on your own. And if you're seeking and open to Him, the Holy Spirit will always be showing you more.

So we want to focus on this—the hope that God gives us for our times of tears. No matter what fire or flood you are going through now, you can still be living in great expectation!

James wrote, "Dear brothers and sisters, when troubles of any kind come your way, consider it an opportunity for great joy" (James 1:2).

There's trouble ahead! What an opportunity!

Have you said or thought that recently?

No, I haven't either.

Trouble and joy. We might think that it is not possible for those two to live in the same space. During the times we might describe as the lowest point of our lives or the most painful or the most trying, we do not expect to find any thread of joy.

But as we open our eyes to see from the perspective of Christ's kingdom of light, we do find that our tears will water our joy. God's promises for our toughest times do, indeed, give us cause for rejoicing. For those whose thoughts are fixed on God, trouble and joy do live together in hope.

MORE: Psalm 1:6; Psalm 13; Nahum 1:7

GOD WILL BE AT WORK

And we know that in all things God works for the good of those who love him, who have been called according to his purpose.
- **ROMANS 8:28 NIV** -

The title of this meditation might seem strange. Can we say that suffering is God at work?

No, but God is at work *in* our times of tears. One of the promises we have is that in spite of pain and trouble, God is always working for our good.

This is so much more than simple optimism or "looking for the silver lining" or "looking on the bright side." The silver lining isn't always visible. The darkness may be so heavy we cannot see any bright side. But we will still hold to the hope, to the confident trust that in spite of our circumstances, Romans 8:28 is reality. God is doing what He said He would do— work for our good in everything.

Romans 8:28 is such a familiar verse and appears in so many places and ways these days that I even hesitated to use it here. We can recite it glibly. And I'm afraid its power too often rolls past us just as quickly as the words roll off our tongues. So today let's take some time to meditate deeply on this statement in Romans 8 and ask ourselves: Do my outlook and my living prove that I believe this?

Look at the confidence that Paul's words show: *And we know.* There's no wondering where God is, no speculating whether or not God has a purpose in whatever is happening to us. Paul *knew*. And our hope can *know*. When we know the reality, doesn't it affect our thinking, feeling, and actions? If we know God is working for our good, how does that change how we see the troubles currently attacking us?

We know God works in *all things*. It's easy to give praise and thanks to God for the good things in our lives. But, sisters and brothers, He is always present and working in the struggles of our lives, too. If you, like me, have doubted that it's possible to follow Paul's advice to "Always be joyful," this hope is key: Even in our most painful moments, knowing that God has promised to bring about something good is a reason for joy.

He is working *for our good*. Again, we must check our thinking. Are we apt to think that trouble comes upon us as punishment? That we must suffer because we deserve it? Tears can come as a result of our own sin or wrong choice, and God does use suffering sometimes to get us back on His path. Suffering and pain are products of our human inheritance in a world poisoned by the enemy of God, but even so, God's power works for the good of those who love Him.

This promise is not just a catchy saying to give a positive spin to things. These words from the heavenly Father to you, His child, can change your life if your hope stands solidly on this promise.

Long before Paul penned Romans 8:28, David declared his belief in the same promise. He wrote,

> The LORD will work out his plans for my life—for your faithful love, O LORD, endures forever. (Psalm138:8)

We hear the reason for David's hope: God's love endures forever. Going back to Romans 8, we find the passage that says nothing will ever separate us from God's love. Trouble or disaster in our lives does not mean He no longer loves us. As a matter of fact, God cares deeply about our heartbreak. He is "full of tenderness and mercy" (James 5:11).

Knowing that God's love will always be acting for us can calm our worries about tomorrow. We certainly won't always feel it. We won't always see it. But this is reality in the privileged place we now stand: God will always be working for our good.

We'll never need to ask, "Where is God in this?" or, "Does God care about what is happening?" He will always be there, He will always care about the anguish of our souls, and He'll always be working for the good of His children.

His love will never quit.

MORE: Psalm 100:5; Romans 8:31, 38, 39

❧ AT WORK IN US ❧

*We can rejoice, too, when we run into problems and trials, for
we know that they help us develop endurance.*

- **ROMANS 5:3** -

Read the verse above. Then, quick, tell me—
what's the verse just before it?

Perhaps you knew the answer, but if not, you
might be surprised to find that this verse about joy
in problems and trials comes immediately after
the verse about standing in a place of undeserved
privilege and looking forward to the future with
confidence and joy!

Again, this is so contrary to the thinking of our
Western culture. Privilege, joy, and confidence—
linked with problems and trials. I have much to learn
about this. But I long to know and live more fully in
my privilege, so I want to learn more.

I'm certainly not going to pretend to know all the
things God has planned for you, His child. Scripture
gives us the promise, and the ways in which God
accomplishes that promise are varied and often
surprising. Many times the good that God is bringing
about is unseen by our eyes.

But may I share some things I have observed and
several Scriptures that do give us more detail?

God's Word tells us that good things can happen
in us during our times of suffering. God uses our
hard times to strengthen and mature His children.

Trials and testing (of all kinds) give opportunity for endurance, faith, perseverance, character, and hope to grow. In that opportunity is cause for joy. In James 1:2-4, we read that ultimately, these traits, especially endurance, make us "perfect" and "complete."

God may also use hard times to teach us new things as we struggle along a rocky road. Deuteronomy 8 lists part of Moses' instructions to the people of Israel who had been wandering in the wilderness for forty years. The "wilderness" for them wasn't only geographical—they had been through much suffering, testing, and grief. God used the wilderness experience to teach them humility and dependence on Him. He was the one who had brought them through. They had not done it on their own; they could not do it on their own. Through their hard journey, they had seen God's power, care, and faithfulness to His promise. They had lived in Egypt for 400 years, but now God was teaching them about a new relationship with Him.

Our heavenly Father might also use suffering and trials to purge things from our lives that need to go. He is constantly refining, correcting, and cleansing us. In Daniel's visions of the future, he was told that persecution would come to God's people, but there was also hope for that time: "In this way, they will be refined and cleansed and made pure until the time of the end" (Daniel 11:35). Don't we all need more refining?

In Psalm 66:8-12, the songwriter recalls some of the history of his people. They went through "fire and flood, but [God] brought us to a place of great abundance." I know that when we are hurting it's difficult to look through the pain to what might lie beyond, but our hope can know that God's plan is to bring us to that place of great abundance. Might it be great abundance of joy? Abundance of love? Abundance of peace? Abundance of compassion? Abundance of patience? Abundance of gratitude?

Whatever the "great abundance" is, I look forward to it. Our hope holds on to the promise that God has a storehouse of goodness for us. We hear the hope of blessings in spite of trouble in Psalm 23 when the psalmist speaks of feasts in the presence of enemies. God's blessings abound, even in the presence of opposition and trials that come against us.

There is reason to rejoice when we meet problems and trials. God will be doing good things in us.

MORE: Psalm 28:7, 8; Isaiah 48:10; Peter 1:6, 7

⚝ AT WORK THROUGH US ⚝

Through suffering, our bodies continue to share in the death of Jesus, so that the life of Jesus may also be seen in our bodies.

- 2 CORINTHIANS 4:10 -

God will use our trials and pain to work for good in the lives of others.

I was traveling with six friends when one of our cars broke down on the freeway, and we needed help. A tow truck soon arrived, but the driver made it clear that he was not happy to be called out that evening. Grumpy, dirty (he'd come from work), and abrupt, he cut off my questions and made no offer to help with anything other than the towing. *Oh, Lord,* I thought, *we need help, but why did You have to send us this one?*

Our group had another car available, but there were seven of us, so two had to ride in the tow truck. And over the next ninety miles to our destination, we discovered that it wasn't us who really needed help that night—it was our grumpy driver. The man had many worries and frustrations roiling in his mind, and the conversation in the cab that evening slowly drew out his concerns. By the end of our ride, a new spirit had settled in him. It was my car that broke down and stranded seven women, but *he* was the one who needed encouragement that night. It was a good night! Yes, I can say that. The memory of it even brings a smile. God used our misfortune to touch that harried life. We saw a change in that man. My car took four days to repair, but I was content.

It may also be that while we are going through pain and tears, God is forging a gift to bestow on us— new tools to help us serve others. Does that sound strange to you? But out of our experience comes compassion for others who might go through the same hardship. We understand what they are experiencing. We know how the enemy can plot to take advantage of our situation. We know the discouragements, the pain, the fear, the doubts—we've been through it!

Many years ago, a friend was seriously injured in a car-motorcycle accident. For most of that summer, she lay unconscious between life and death in the intensive care unit, and I was with her family many times as they sat and waited and prayed and waited and prayed. It was a difficult summer.

I must confess that before that experience, I never gave much thought to the family and loved ones who pray and wait in hospital rooms. But as I lived through those long days and nights, I learned compassion for those who surround the patient. Ever since that long hospital stay, my prayers are for the family as much as they are for the one lying in bed.

While we are still in the middle of these trying times or battles, helping others might be the last thing on our mind. We can't even imagine it. But God may have plans for us to use what we're learning.

What suffering are you enduring now? What hard battles are being fought? Whether you feel it or not, recognize it or not, God may have plans for you in the future, plans for you to use whatever you are learning now to help others who must go forth onto the same battlefield.

Paul wrote that God has given us all gifts and we are to use them well to serve each other. Is it possible that from our hard times we are given this gift—the ability to be Christ to someone else? Could God be working for good to come out of your pain by equipping you to encourage and support others along the way?

MORE: 2 Corinthians 1:3-5; 1 Peter 4:13

 **A LIGHT SHINING**

My grace is all you need. My power works best in weakness.
- 2 CORINTHIANS 12:9 -

Let's go again to one of the familiar accounts in Daniel and watch as Daniel's three friends are bound and then thrown into a fire so hot that they should have died instantly. They were being put to death because they had refused to bow down to the statue of the king. They trusted that God had the power to save them, but they declared that even if He did not save them from the fire, they would never bow to anyone but God.

So they were thrown into the furnace. Yet they did not perish, and when the king peered through the flames, he saw them walking around, unbound. He called to them and asked them to come out, and when they stepped out of the fire, not a hair had been lost in the flames. Their clothes were not touched and did not even smell of smoke.

King Nebuchadnezzar was convinced. "There is no other god who can rescue like this!" he said. He was so impressed with their God and their faith that he promoted them to higher positions in the kingdom. (And remember, they were foreigners in the land!) He also issued a decree that no one in his kingdom could speak a word against their Almighty God. They influenced the entire country with their stand of faith and improved their own earthly fortunes as well.

Our suffering and trials have effects that work for Christ's kingdom.

Jesus told His disciples that persecution would come, and they would be arrested and brought to trial before the authorities. "But this is an opportunity," He said. "An opportunity to tell them about me" (Luke 21:12, 13 AP). We may not be persecuted and dragged into court, but our steadfastness in hard times, while we are going through pain and tears, can stand as witness to Christ. Like Daniel's three friends who declared their trust in God to save them, we have an opportunity to stand firm in our hope and thus give evidence of God's power and His goodness even in our own fiery ordeal.

We bear the name of Christ. We claim to believe in a living God. Whether we go through personal trials or are persecuted because of our faith, the manner in which we walk through the dark valleys will tell others about our God.

Often, our lives reveal far more about the God of all hope than our words do.

"Let your light shine," Jesus tells us, "so that others will praise your heavenly Father." The light shines brightest in the darkness.

MORE: Matthew 5:44, 45; 2 Corinthians 5:15; 1 Peter 2:9, 12

THERE WILL BE POWER

*And I trust that my life will bring honor to Christ,
whether I live or die.*
- PHILIPPIANS 1:20 -

King Nebuchadnezzar had been furious with Shadrach, Meshach, and Abednego. They had even been given a second chance to bow down and worship his statue, but they had stood steadfast, refusing to worship anyone but their God. He ordered the furnace heated seven times hotter than usual, and he waited to see the sentence of death carried out.

I want to stand that firm in the face of fire. I want my light to shine brightly as I walk through a dark valley. I want to always bring honor to Christ in how I handle testing. But there are times I can't even return a blessing for an insult, as Jesus instructs us to do. I fail the test. How will I hold up when the fire is turned up seven times hotter?

Peter failed, too. After he had promised to die with Jesus, he deserted at the critical moment. But something happened to Peter, and it is in his letters to Christians who were suffering terrible persecution (they were being thrown to the lions) that we find so much hope and encouragement to stand strong in our trials.

What changed Peter? The power of the Holy Spirit living in him. Once Peter received the gift of the Spirit, he was a changed man.

As Nebuchadnezzar peered through the flames, he was shocked to see the men upright, walking around, free of the ropes that had bound them. They should have disintegrated! Even more astounding was that now there were four men in the flames.

Here is the wonderful promise—we will not be in the furnace or walking through the dark valley alone. Jesus will always keep that promise of being with His disciples forever and wherever. And it is His power that will keep us from disintegrating in the fire and get us through.

> We also pray that you will be strengthened with all his glorious power so you will have all the endurance and patience you need. May you be filled with joy. (Colossians 1:11)

His glorious power. Remember that our King holds *all* power in heaven and earth. That power defeated death. It defeated all spiritual adversaries. It created the universe. And—it strengthens us! Surely that is cause for great joy!

We will not walk by our own strength. Paul wrote in 2 Corinthians 4 that we have the Good News shining in our hearts, but we are only fragile clay jars holding a great treasure. "This makes it clear that our great power is from God, not from ourselves" (2 Corinthians 4:7). Besieged by trouble on every side, he wrote, we might be knocked down, but we will not be destroyed. In our places of weakness and frailty, God's power will surge more powerfully through us.

Here is another change we must make in our thinking. In our culture, personal strength, determination, and self-control are extolled. We've got what it takes, we're told. We've got it in us to handle whatever comes our way. But we've only

EXPANTION OF OUR TEARS

"got it in us" if what we have is the Spirit of Christ.

And at the very darkest times of our lives, in the very hottest fires, it will be His power that will carry us, keep us safe, and get us through.

My hope counts on the fourth man in the fire. He's promised He'll always be there—with His glorious power—and we can always expect Him. That will be our greatest joy in our troubles.

MORE: Psalm 44:5; John 16:33; Ephesians 3:16; 2 Corinthians 12:9, 10

☙ PRIVILEGE! ❧

For you have been given not only the privilege of trusting in Christ but also the privilege of suffering for him.
- **PHILIPPIANS 1:29** -

Whatever hard time you will go through, count it not only as an opportunity for joy but also as a privilege. Another translation says this privilege has been "granted" to us.

This may take some sitting, contemplating, praying, and asking God for understanding.

How can it be that our trials and troubles are a privilege we've been granted? Perhaps you're not experiencing any trouble or hard times now, but that means it's a good time to do that sitting and praying for understanding so that your mind and heart are prepared.

Let's look at the first disciples of Jesus. For them, persecution set in almost immediately after Jesus left this earth. Those early followers of Jesus were "bucking the system." They were Jews, and they were now seen as rebels against the established "church" (to put things in modern context). Take Paul, for example. As he traveled extensively to carry the message of Good News throughout the empire, he often encountered strong and even violent resistance from the Jewish community. In Ephesus, Paul began preaching in the synagogue, but the opposition became so strong that he and the believers left and began holding their meetings in a lecture hall.

So the early believers were persecuted for their faith in Jesus, not only from the non-Jewish world but also from their own religious tradition. In all of the New Testament, the context is that believers are opposed and persecuted from nearly every side. But those believers knew—in a way I fear we do not understand—that this suffering was a privilege.

Peter and other apostles had been teaching and drawing crowds, and the religious high council was furious. They even decided to kill the troublemakers. Their fury was calmed a bit by one Pharisee who advised a more rational approach, but the apostles were still brought in, flogged, and ordered to quit speaking about Jesus. "The apostles left the high council rejoicing that God had counted them worthy to suffer disgrace for the name of Jesus" (Acts 5:41).

Do we count it a privilege to suffer for our King? Would you feel that way if you were flogged? Try to imagine it. Maybe you've had to endure emotional, verbal, or cyber flogging because you've talked about your faith. Were you rejoicing?

Let's not limit this to religious persecution. We might be tempted to think that other types of suffering common to all humanity—like physical distress, disasters, relationship tensions, emotional issues, and bereavement—would not be "suffering for Him."

I think all our suffering is for the sake of Jesus' name. Everything we do, we're to do "as unto the Lord." We are standing as witnesses for our Lord in the way we handle our bereavement, the loss of our home to a tornado, the cancer invading our body, or the rebellious child who says she hates us.

In all of those circumstances, evil forces of the unseen realm are coming against us, not just to harm us individually, but to attack Christ's kingdom and His people. It really makes no difference what kind of fire or flood threatens us; we are a target of those spiritual forces because we stand with and for Christ. The ruler of the dark kingdom would love to see our hope in Christ crumble.

Do you see it as a privilege to be counted as one of His? Will you rejoice when you are granted the privilege of suffering as one of His? It will be an opportunity for you to show the world what a difference Christ can make in life.

MORE: Acts 5:40-42; Acts 1:8; Romans 8:16, 17

COMFORT

Trust your lives to the God who created you, for he will never fail you.

– 1 PETER 4:19 –

As we face the future, we know that all kinds of trouble and pain will come to our lives. It may be any kind of loss: spiritual battles, physical problems, persecution because we bear the name of Christ, evil that tears holes in our lives, or the consequences of our own sin. We have not differentiated in these meditations, because the promises of God apply to all of our trials.

So no matter what will grieve you in the future, causing stress and pain and threatening to swamp your boat, God's promises will hold true. We have these hopes for our hard times.

There may come a time when you are not able to look beyond today's pain to even imagine the promises coming to fruition. You might not think you can hold on for even "a little while." Pain numbs us. Darkness can be so heavy we can't see even a tiny speck of light. The roar of conflict and battle might shut out voices of encouragement and hope.

If times like that come, take the Psalm prayer for this chapter as your own. Ask for God's comfort. Ask for your hope to be renewed by His promises. And then take up His Word and look for those promises.

With the Spirit's guidance, you'll find the words that bring you the most peace, but as a start, I'd like to share some of my favorites. These are Scriptures that have brought light into my darkest times.

- The LORD is close to the brokenhearted; he rescues those whose spirits are crushed. (Psalm 34:18)

- O God, you are my God. I earnestly search for you. My soul thirsts for you... I cling to you; your strong right hand holds me securely. (Psalm 63:1, 8)

- I wait quietly before God, for my victory comes from him. He alone is my rock and my salvation, my fortress where I will never be shaken. (Psalm 62:1,2)

- I lie in the dust; revive me by your word. (Psalm 119:25)

- Unfailing love surrounds those who trust in the LORD. (Psalm 32:10)

- My enemies will retreat when I call to you for help. This I know: God is on my side! (Psalm 56:9)

- For you have rescued me from death; you have kept my feet from slipping. So now I can walk in your presence, O God, in your life-giving light. (Psalm 56:13)

- He also turns deserts into pools of water. (Psalm 107:35)

- Let my soul be at rest again, for the LORD has been good to me. He has saved me from death, my eyes from tears, my feet from stumbling. And so I walk in the LORD's presence as I live here on earth! (Psalm 116:7-9)

- Yet I still dare to hope when I remember this: The faithful love of the LORD never ends! His mercies never cease. (Lamentations 3:21, 22)

- To comfort all who mourn... to bestow on them a crown of beauty instead of ashes, the oil of joy instead of mourning, and a garment of praise instead of a spirit of despair. They will be called oaks of righteousness, a planting of the LORD for the display of his splendor. (Isaiah 61:2, 3 NIV)

- I, yes I, am the one who comforts you. (Isaiah 51:12)

- I have called you by name; you are mine. When you go through deep waters, I will be with you. When you go through rivers of difficulty, you will not drown. When you walk through the fire of oppression, you will not be burned up; the flames will not consume you... You are precious to me... Do not be afraid, for I am with you. (Isaiah 43:1, 2, 4, 5)

- Don't be afraid, for I am with you. Don't be discouraged, for I am your God. I will strengthen you and help you. I will hold you up with my victorious right hand. (Isaiah 41:10)

Find the words in Scripture that speak hope and peace to you. Perhaps you'll want to mark them or copy them into a journal of some kind. Then anchor your boat firmly to them. When the storms come (and we know they will), trust Him to hold you.

He will not fail you.

⟞ HE WILL ⟝

The Lord knows how to rescue godly people from their trials.
- 2 PETER 2:9 -

The above verse is really all we need to know! Right? This is the God we trust to save us. He knows how to rescue us from the fire and the flood. *And He will.*

"I want to know when this will end! When will I be through this?" My friend was joking, and I knew it. We were talking about our hope in times of trouble, and the first thought that popped into her head was that question. That same day, someone else referred to the promise that "Soon God will crush Satan under your feet." What is "soon"? That is the question! We want the battle to be over.

It is an urgent question for us when we are in the midst of the fire or when we are fighting a battle. In the Psalms, we often hear David pounding on God's door and (I imagine) shouting, "How long, Lord? How long is this going to go on?"

We don't know. We aren't given exact times.

But we are given the confident promise that there *will* be rescue and that good things *will* come:

> So after you have suffered a little while, he will restore, support, and strengthen you, and he will place you on a firm foundation. (1 Peter 5:10)

Jesus left us with this word of hope: "But take heart, because I have overcome the world" (John 16:33). We're still in this world and still facing many trials and tribulations, but Jesus' power is greater than any power those troubles can exert on our lives. We are not bound to be prisoners or slaves to the suffering. We need not be paralyzed by hard times. His power working in us is the same power that raised a man from the dead—and that will one day resurrect us to immortality! That power can surely take us through any trouble we may meet on the path ahead.

As we face the future and the certainty of tears, these are important things we know: We are very precious to God. Jesus has promised to always walk with us through whatever we meet. To help us. To restore, support, and strengthen us. To prepare us feasts, even in the middle of trouble. And to put us, once again, back on a firm foundation.

Trouble may plague us here, but it will not rule us.

MORE: Psalm 56:9, 10; 1 Corinthians 1:8, 9; 1 John 4:4

🌿 LIGHT AND MOMENTARY 🌿

Yet what we suffer now is nothing compared to the glory he will reveal to us later.

- ROMANS 8:18 -

Think about everything you've been through.

The writer of Hebrews wrote these words to the early Christians who were holding on to their hope in spite of terrible suffering. He listed some specifics: They were ridiculed, beaten, and thrown into jail. They had lost much—probably not only property but also jobs, social standing, friends, and influence. And they suffered not only for themselves but also with others going through the same things. Yet they "accepted it with joy." They were looking ahead to better things that would last forever.

Jesus talked of joy in persecution, too. Persecution will come if we choose to follow Him. He added this: "Be happy when it does! Be happy when people hate you because you follow me! Dance for joy!"

Our King sounds radical, doesn't He?

He had more to say. He promised blessings from God now and a great reward in the future.

We will all experience different kinds of suffering in our lives. Our times of tears will be from varied causes. But one thing we children of God will all meet: persecution because we follow

Jesus. It might be persecution in violent form—
Jesus said the time will come when people seek to
kill His disciples and think they are doing work for
God. That's happening today. Jesus' followers will
be arrested and brought to court because of what
they believe; that's happening today. Those who
stand for Christ's truth will be ridiculed, called all
kinds of names, and ostracized. That's happening
every day.

Peter encouraged disciples to stand firm because
there will be much praise, honor, and glory for you
if your faith remains strong through the trials (1
Peter 1:7). Don't skim over those three things.
Consider what might be waiting for you: Praise.
Honor. Glory. I can't imagine how glorious all that
will be, can you?

Paul wrote that anything we have to suffer on
this earth is *nothing* compared to what our Father
is going to show us someday.

Jesus knows this! He knows all about things
we can't see, those things we will only know later.
He knows what's waiting for us, what God has in
store. We can't imagine it, but it must be amazing if
Jesus tells us to dance for joy when we're suffering
for heaven's sake. These earthly trials must truly be
nothing compared to what is coming.

Hold tightly to your anchor. For those who do,
there are blessings now and more rewards coming!

We'll take a more thorough look at heavenly rewards later, but for now,

> Rejoice in our confident hope.
> Be patient in trouble,
> and keep on praying.
> (Romans 12:12)

MORE: Luke 6:22, 23; 2 Corinthians 4:17; Hebrews 10:32-36

PRAYER TO STAY STRONG:

My health may fail and my spirit grow weak, but you, O Lord, will remain the strength of my heart.

— **PSALM 73:26 AP** —

STAYING
STRONG

 **ENDURE!**

So let's not get tired of doing what is good.

- GALATIANS 6:9 -

"Three times. I almost quit three times. It was so hard. I said, 'That's it. I am done with this. No more.' But then I'd get up the next morning and do a bit more—and now look at this. Isn't it beautiful?"

My friend's hands caressed the surface of the jigsaw puzzle on the table, now complete, a leaf-shaped scene of winter on the lake.

Okay, I understand that if you are not a

puzzle lover, you probably can't identify with this illustration. But please try!

She went on to tell me how she had struggled to finish that "ridiculous" challenge. Even for her, with years of experience and love of puzzling, the jigsaw had been frustrating. But she had not given up. Her husband had also joined the battle, offering encouragement and help—and they had won!

Don't take my friend's experience lightly because it was "only" a jigsaw puzzle. Her wrangling with a thousand small, perplexing pieces is a parable for us as we journey through this world.

We do get tired, don't we? We get discouraged. We might even get to the point where we throw up our hands and say, "Lord, this is just too hard. I can't do it."

What is it that you are tempted to give up on?

Being kind to that neighbor who seems bent on criticizing everything you do?

Forgiving your spouse?

Continuing the ministry you were called to that is encountering so many hurdles?

Learning to be patient?

Praying for that hard heart that has not yielded one iota?

Resisting that bait the enemy has put in front of you, promising it's yours for the taking?

Leading the Bible study where attendance is inconsistent and dwindling?

Living out something the Spirit has shown you must happen in your life?

Or the opposite—rooting out from your life something the Spirit has told you must go?

The puzzle parable isn't quite finished. An interesting thing happened with the puzzle. After my friend's triumph, I passed it on to another friend, who took one look at it, pronounced it "too scary" to start, and put it away in a closet. Yes, it is a scary-*looking* puzzle. (I still have it, and if you're an enthusiast and want to tackle it, I'll happily send it to you.)

Sometimes we do the same thing when we look at the road ahead and know the route Christ would have us take. We decide it's "too scary." It will be too difficult to do the right thing. Too tough to make our way through the daunting task ahead. Too strenuous to climb the mountain looming in our path. As we face tomorrow, we're afraid that to take Jesus' way will just be too hard.

When we believe in Christ and become children of God, our heavenly Father doesn't send a chariot to whisk us away and take us home to Him immediately. We are still here, still in the midst of the agonies of this world that touch every one of our lives in various ways and intensities. All of us, regardless of how many years we've lived, have already learned the truth of Jesus' words that we will have trials and troubles in this life.

But no matter what we've already been through and no matter what the road into the future might look like, we won't give up. We must not give up.

In His Word to us, our heavenly Father repeatedly gives us words of encouragement:

Fight the good fight for the true faith. (1 Timothy 6:12)

Be strong and immovable. Always work enthusiastically for the LORD. (1 Corinthians 15:58)

Stand firm against [your enemy, the devil], and be strong in your faith. (1 Peter 5:9)

Love never gives up, never loses faith, is always hopeful, and endures through every circumstance. (1 Corinthians 13:7)

Rejoice in our confident hope. Be patient in trouble, and keep on praying. (Romans 12:12)

Run with endurance the race God has set before us. (Hebrews 12:1)

Run to win! (1 Corinthians 9:24)

Our first question is, *How?* How do we keep going? When we don't feel strong, immovable, and confident at all—just scared, tired, and weak—how do we not give up?

The Spirit has answers for us in God's Word. We are not helpless or hopeless. Let's hear what He has to say.

MORE: Psalm 34:2; Galatians 6:7-10; 2 Timothy 3:16, 17

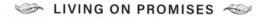 **LIVING ON PROMISES**

Let us hold tightly without wavering to the hope we affirm,
for God can be trusted to keep his promise.
— HEBREWS 10:23 —

The title above was not my first choice. My preferred title was: "Know His Promises, Believe His Promises, Pray His Promises, Because He Keeps His Promises." But you see the problem with that. Much too long. Finding the perfect title has always been a challenge for me.

Perhaps I should include a disclaimer even before the title: I don't have all the answers. I do not always stand strong and immovable. Discouragement sometimes wrestles me to the ground, and I lie there in the dust for a bit. My life has had its dark days. We've all had them. But I do want to share with you some of the helps for my own hope. Your hope will find its own shining lifelines in God's Word. Grab them and hold tight.

Those lifelines are God's promises to us, our heavenly Father's words of love to let us know what He can and will do. That's why He's given us His Word: so that we *can* know. The Scriptures are a direct communication to us, even more direct than any love letter you've ever received, more than any text, phone call, email, or Facebook message. The Holy Spirit uses the Word to connect us to God's thoughts. When you seek His voice and heart there, you will always find Him.

So, first of all, before we can hold tightly to God's promises, we'll have to know what they are. How else can we have any hope?

Let's remind ourselves that the hope spoken of in Scripture is not merely wishing that something might happen or be true. Hope is the certainty, the *expectation,* that what is promised will come to pass. It is *seeing* the fulfillment of the promise. (Maybe this book series should be called "Hope Sees"?)

Let's go back to the book of Daniel. These words are from Daniel's prayer:

> You always fulfill your covenant and keep
> your promises of unfailing love to those
> who love you and obey your commands.
> (Daniel 9:4)

This is the foundation of all our hope—that God keeps His promises and holds fast to His covenant with us. If this is not true, then every hope we have is futile. We cannot move forward with courage, joy, or peace. We'll always be wondering if God will ignore us, decide that today's not a good day to come through on His word, or, maybe, even be angry if we have the audacity to ask for what He promised. If God can't be trusted to do what He says He'll do, then the future will be depressing at best, terrifying at worst.

But God can be trusted! The apostle Paul opened his letter to Titus by proclaiming confidence in the truth of eternal life, "which God—who does not lie—promised them before the world began" (Titus 1:2).

God's Word holds—for all of the world's history, and before, and beyond. We can trust it.

An interesting thing about Daniel's prayer is that it is for his nation, a confession of their failure to keep their part of the covenant with God. Daniel pleads for mercy and forgiveness for a wayward people who have not kept their promises to God. Why would God then keep His covenant with them? He would and does, because a part of God's covenant with His people is that when we fail, confession and repentance will be met with God's mercy and forgiveness.

So we can trust Him. Trust Him to do what He says He will do. Trust Him to be our God. Trust

Him to be who He says He is—a God of love and compassion and mercy and power, who works for those who love Him.

The promises He has made to us will keep us moving ahead and will give us confidence, courage, guidance, and comfort along the way. To gain all that, we'll need to know what He has said. And we'll need to act on the promise. If the promises of God are bridges of hope He has built to carry us forward, then faith is our action of walking forward, believing that the bridges will hold us. Faith is living according to what God says is reality. He has put the bridges there for us when we can't see how to keep going, but we'll never get anywhere if we don't go ahead and move.

We can also pattern our prayers on the promises. God has promised His strength will help us; we can pray for strength. We have His promise for a new heart; we can pray for His miraculous change of our old self. He's promised to carry us every day; sometimes, all we can do is utter a few words, begging to be carried.

So, back to the problem of my title. It says so little of what I want to encourage you to do. Some will be put off by it, and some might scoff. After all, in our modern day, we have learned not to live on promises.

But at the same time, the title says it all: This is the way to live, children of God. We build our lives on what He's promised us for today, tomorrow, and the past. We ask Him to be true to His Word. And we move ahead, knowing He will be true to His Word.

MORE: Deuteronomy 7:9; 2 Timothy 2:13; Hebrews 6:17

 **KEY CLOTHING**

Clothe yourselves with the presence of the Lord Jesus Christ.
- **ROMANS 13:14** -

I backed into my grandson's car. Both cars still bear the scars.

Yes, I have decades of driving experience. Yes, I know how to use my rear-view mirrors. Yes, I even have one of those backup assist screens on my dashboard. Yes, I knew his car was parked behind and slightly to the left of mine.

Nevertheless, I started my car, put 'er in reverse, and in a few yards, heard the crunch and felt my car jerk to a stop.

I repeat, I knew his car was back there. It always is. That's his usual parking spot. But for a crucial three seconds, I forgot that fact.

We spent an entire chapter celebrating the fact that we aren't traveling alone. But how often do we forget this fact? We forget that Jesus has said He will always be with us. Jesus does not forget us, but we forget Him. We forget that He travels with us. We forget that it is only His strength that carries us through. We forget that He has said His power is greatest during times we feel the weakest, the most discouraged, and the most troubled. We forget all of the promises He has made to His children.

Okay, I confess, my inattention to the crucial fact of a car behind me was born out of distraction. I was too busy checking my hair in the mirror to remember the presence of that car.

And isn't that what we do spiritually? In the course of our day, how often are we too busy looking at our own reflection—looking to ourselves, going to our own strength, wisdom, and resourcefulness—to realize that God is right here with us, offering all of *His* strength, wisdom, and resourcefulness? We struggle along on our own steam, and we forget that He has promised to get us through every situation we encounter in the journey.

> Let us run with endurance the race God has set before us. We do this by keeping our eyes on Jesus, the champion who initiates and perfects our faith. (Hebrews 12:1, 2)

We falter, my friends, when we look only at ourselves and forget God's presence in our lives and His promises to us. What consequences do we suffer?

Confusion. Wringing our hands. Fear. Loneliness. A feeling of helplessness and hopelessness. And unhappy crashes that leave scars. Can you add to the list?

How different life can be when we keep our eyes on our Champion, the one who has promised to help us through everything.

The opening verse from Romans is taken from a passage that talks about the urgency of living decent lives because time is rushing on, the end of the world's history is approaching, and children of God need to "put on the shining armor of right living" (Romans 13:12). Clothing ourselves with the presence of Christ helps us fight the sinful desires within us.

Putting on such "clothing" every morning will help us in every aspect of our day.

Dressing ourselves every morning is essential. We aren't going to head into the day without being properly attired for whatever is on our schedule, whether we're going to sit at a desk in the office, mow the lawn, or put a new roof on a house. It's even more important for us to clothe ourselves spiritually. Many passages of Scripture talk of "putting on" essential wear for the day, and this verse from Romans summarizes all of them: Clothe yourself with the presence of Jesus.

Daily, we cover ourselves, wrap ourselves, outfit ourselves with the presence of Jesus. We make a habit of it every morning as soon as we come out of sleep. We dress ourselves with His presence, and we wear that blessed, powerful, gracious, compassionate presence through everything that comes that day because, believe me, that clothing is the most appropriate choice for everything we're going to be doing.

The more we remember to clothe ourselves with the consciousness of His presence, the more strength and endurance we'll have for the race.

And we'll have fewer crashes, too.

MORE: Psalm 63:6-8; Psalm 139:1-10; John 15:4, 5

∽ DEEP ROOTS ∾

Then Christ will make his home in your hearts as you trust in him. Your roots will grow down into God's love and keep you strong.

– **EPHESIANS 3:17** –

In my family, I have a reputation for having a black thumb. As much as I love green, growing things, I can't keep houseplants alive. For a number of years, I tried; I would buy new plants, enjoy them for their short life span, then replace each when it died. But plants always dying on me began to feel depressing, so I finally gave up. In my flower beds, anything that sprouted unplanned and bloomed cheerfully on its own was welcomed, celebrated, and allowed to stay.

So maybe the poor, crooked tree was doomed from the minute I started digging a hole in the front yard. Someone had given the tree to me, and I thought it would be a grand addition to the lawn; I have memories of two other large trees that stood there in a previous generation.

My optimism and enthusiasm were high as I dug, and the tree did survive for a number of years, growing tall and slender. But one summer after a windstorm roared through, we looked out to see the tree lying flat on the grass.

I saw, then, that it had almost no root system. Whether that was a result of my not digging a hole deep enough, I do not know. It could also have been because the soil here has a great deal of clay—one of the reasons I had not dug very deep.

There's a lesson for me. I may not know how to plant a tree properly, but I do know that I must have deep roots myself, or I won't survive the storms.

How do deep roots keep us strong? Look at plants. The root system is essential for their growth; roots are the channel through which water and nutrients flow from the soil to all parts of the plant. Roots also keep the plant securely fixed in its place. You see the spiritual parallel. Sending our roots deep into the love of God nourishes all parts of our lives, grows us, and anchors us.

We may acknowledge that truth, but *how?* How

do we send our roots deep into His love?

Think for a moment how you "put down roots" in a community. The answer lies in *relationship*. Deep roots are a result of deep relationship.

The opening verse comes from a passage that shows a progression of relationship. We believe in Christ. Christ comes to make His home with us. We learn to trust Him. Our roots grow down into His love and *keep us strong.*

It is much like the progression of human relationships of trust and love. We constantly, daily, in varied ways, seek out God. The more you get to know Him, the more you trust. Those who seek God will find Him. That's another promise we can count on.

As you enter into, develop, and pursue this relationship with God, you will experience more and more of His love. I can't tell you how you will experience that love, but you will!

As I type that statement, I have to stop in amazement. The all-powerful Creator of the universe desires to have a relationship with me? That is almost unbelievable! Yet we do believe it because He says it is so. We are taking our nourishment from and anchoring our lives in His solid love for us.

Deep roots will save us from unhappy crashes that leave scars. We'll be stronger. We'll know more peace and courage. And there's an amazing promise that follows these verses in Ephesians about deep roots and relationship. Verse 19 of chapter 3 says that as we experience more and more of the love of Christ, we are being "made complete with all the fullness of life and power that comes from God."

Fullness of life and power from God. Can you imagine what that might look like? I don't want to imagine—I want to *know*. My life hasn't reached that peak yet, but I'm putting down my roots.

MORE: Colossians 2:7; 2 Thessalonians 2:16, 17; 1 Peter 5:10

 **LIFE ONLY BY THE SPIRIT**

Let us follow the Spirit's leading in every part of our lives.
- GALATIANS 5:25 -

Brothers and sisters in the family of God, there's only one way for us to go on into the future: following the leading of the Spirit of God.

The life of the Holy Spirit within us is how God the Father and Jesus Christ have come to live with us. The Spirit's purpose and work are so far-reaching that we cannot cover it all in one or a dozen or even three dozen meditations. Back in Chapter 4 (We Aren't Traveling Alone), we listed many of the purposes of the Holy Spirit within us. Perhaps the one that includes almost all of them is the statement from Romans 8:6: "Letting the Spirit control your mind leads to life and peace."

Life and peace. What we all desire, right?

But there's a war going on within: the war between the Spirit of God (who will bring that life and peace) and the old, sinful nature that Satan has corrupted. That war is going to be constant until God's purposes reach their final fulfillment and we are rid of that old nature forever.

So, just as we have a choice whether or not we clothe ourselves with the presence of Christ, we have a choice between these two forces within. Are we going to follow the Spirit's leading? Or are we are going to capitulate to the old nature, the one that brings out the worst in us. Galatians 5:19-21 lists the results of following the desires of our sinful nature. I won't list them all, but some that I suspect we all battle are hostility, quarreling, jealousy, anger, selfishness, and envy. (If you're free of all those, go ahead and skip to the next meditation.)

We have the choice, but all of the power to overcome that old nature lies with the Holy Spirit. The power is His. Christ died to break the power of sin in our lives. His Spirit in us is now the greater of the two forces. I am so grateful for our heavenly Father's assurance to us:

> Therefore, dear brothers and sisters, you
> have no obligation to do what your sinful

nature urges you to do. (Romans 8:12)

We are no longer slaves to sin. (Romans 6:6)

Nothing else in my life was able to break that slavery!

God's power works through the Spirit in His children, and as we peer down the path into the future, His promise is that the path of the Spirit will be a path where we'll be taught, given wisdom, guided along the right way, and changed. Along that path, we'll be given strength, comfort, and power.

Stop and go back to the previous paragraph. Read it again—slowly—and let it all soak in...

Don't you want to jump up and run down that path?

MORE: Ephesians 6:10; Philippians 2:13; Hebrews 13:21; 1 John 4:4

 **OUR PRAYERS MATTER**

Never stop praying.
- **1 THESSALONIANS 5:17** -

Satan, you know, is a liar. Deception is his strategy, and his frequent target is our emotions. So when you pray and you feel as though your prayers are not heard, don't you believe it!

Daniel certainly had his ups and downs emotionally. His prayer, found in Daniel 9:1-19, is heavy with his sorrow, repentance, and entreaties. Three times he pleads with God to hear his prayer, to listen, and to act. Have you uttered prayers like that? When you seem to be pounding on a door and no one is answering?

During one vision, the heavenly messenger sent to Daniel assured him, "Since the first day you began to pray for understanding and to humble yourself before your God, your request has been heard in heaven." Another time, he was told that "the moment you began praying," there was action in heaven (Daniel 9:23 and 10:12).

In God's Word to us, He gives us assurance just as clear and forceful as the message to Daniel. Try to read these verses as though you've never heard them before:

> Don't worry about anything; instead, pray about everything. Tell God what you need, and thank him for all he has done. Then you will experience God's peace, which exceeds anything we can understand. His peace will guard your hearts and minds as you live in Christ Jesus. (Philippians 4:6, 7)

That's a ringing declaration from your God, just as emphatic as if an angelic messenger were standing by your chair right now. *Don't worry about anything.* (I'd like to bold and underline that and put it all in caps.) *Pray about everything.*

And while we might be so impressed by Daniel's prayers bringing a response from heaven, our prayers following these guidelines will do something every bit as miraculous as the results of Daniel's prayers: *We'll have peace of mind and heart.*

Or if we need wisdom: "Ask our generous God, and he will give it to you" (James 1:5). He won't be scolding, either. He's generous, our God. He wants us to lean on what He knows, not on what we know.

Whatever we need, we can ask for. He will supply all that we need.

We can pray for others, too. In his letter to Timothy, Paul recommends praying for "all people," interceding—wait, have you ever thought about what interceding means? It's intervening on behalf of someone, stepping in between opposing parties, or acting on behalf of someone who needs help. *You have that opportunity.*

This is one more hope we have as we go forward in our journey, one hope that keeps us strong: Our prayers do matter.

Prayer is so important that the Holy Spirit picks up for us when we are at a loss as to how to pray. He is not going to let that connection with the heavenly Father drop. He'll pray if we can't!

Our prayers matter in more ways than we might know. Praying affects our mindset and our emotions. In almost every verse about prayer, we are also told to be thankful. Thank God for what He has done, thank Him for those people we pray for, thank Him for who He is and what He's promised. Hearts and minds infused with gratefulness are changed.

And then in the Philippians verses above, we come back once again to the peace God has promised, a peace that is beyond anything the world will understand. This peace will stand guard over us.

Prayer focuses our minds on God. It reminds us that He rules and that He holds all power and our future. And what was that verse on the very first page of our meditations together? A perfect peace—for those whose minds stay on their God.

MORE: Psalm 50:15; Romans 12:12; Ephesians 6:18; Colossians 4:2

IMPORTANT BODY BUILDING

So encourage each other and build each other up.
- 1 THESSALONIANS 5:11 -

Many of us may be ignoring and neglecting one of the helps God has given to keep us strong as we go marching into tomorrow. Or perhaps it's just that we are underestimating its power. Many passages about birth-pain times and the end of the world speak of the importance of this one source of help and protection. *Knowing what is ahead,* the Scriptures tell us, *don't stop loving, encouraging, teaching, and counseling each other.*

Since Jesus has left the earth, His power works here through the Holy Spirit, and the Spirit gives us that supernatural connection to other children of God. Through this connection, we sisters and brothers can encourage and build up each other.

Each other.

That's a strange phrase, quickly sounding odd when you say or think it several times. "Each" and "other," coupled together to create a meaning greater than either one or the other.

That's what the Spirit means to do when He connects "each" and "other." Each one of us can draw strength and courage from others. We can instill courage in others. A favorite phrase used by the writers of the New Testament letters is *build up.* The children of God can build each other up with words, counsel, love, patience, compassion, and forgiveness.

Colossians 3:1-17 is a wonderful, heart-warming passage when you read it from the perspective of body building. Many of us (myself included) have often read these verses thinking only of the application they might have to our individual lives. But I encourage you to take time to read it now, and read it as addressed to the body of Christ, the family of the children of God. Here Paul reminds us of our focus as people who have a new life; he talks of new ways to live and (again) new clothes to put on and gives us ruling principles in relating to each other.

Reading these seventeen verses with your Christian brothers and sisters in mind gives a new layer of meaning to verse 17. This is probably a verse you have known since you were a child: "Whatever you do or say, do it as a representative of the Lord Jesus." We memorized that as children to remind us to be careful of our actions. But the verse comes at the end of a passage on how we treat others in the body of Christ. When set in the context of building each other up, these words have a startling meaning: You and I have these relationships with other children of God *as representatives of Jesus.*

Here on earth, in our visible, tangible world, the Spirit works through us—that's *you* and *me*—to build up Christ's body, building courage, love, faith, and peace in each other.

Jude wrote about birth-pain times. His letter opens in an interesting way: He said he was looking forward to writing about the wonderful news of salvation, but instead he found he must write about the importance of standing firm in the truth of the Gospel. In verse 20, he also refers to body building:

But you, dear friends, must build each other
up in your most holy faith, pray in the power
of the Holy Spirit, and await the mercy of our
Lord Jesus Christ, who will bring you eternal
life. In this way, you will keep yourselves
safe in God's love. (Jude 1:20, 21)

Building each other up will keep faith strong in
the body of Christ and keep believers safe within
God's encircling love. (And did you notice the
importance of prayer again?)

How do we build others up? Those first seventeen
verses of Colossians 3 give us a wonderful picture of
the attitudes and actions that foster an atmosphere
where people will be kept safe in God's love. The
first sixteen verses of Ephesians 4 also talk about our
each/other life—being humble, patient, forgiving,
and loving.

The Spirit gives us each a gift—something we
do well, something for which we have a passion,
something that is meant for us to help others.
Your gift was not given to you solely for your own
benefit; it was given to you so you could help me.
Your gift may be the giving of wise advice, it may
be hospitality, it may be the ability to teach well or
to listen with compassion or to be kind to a weary
heart. Whatever ability the Spirit has given you, it
was given "so we can help each other."

Each other.

Each and other. Giving and receiving strength and courage for our journey into tomorrow.

MORE: 1 Corinthians 12:4-7; Ephesians 4:16; Hebrews 10:24, 25; 1 Peter 4:7-10

 TAKE A FIRM STANCE IN TRUTH

You must continue to believe this truth and stand firmly in it.
- COLOSSIANS 1:23 -

As we read the book of Daniel in its entirety, we cannot miss the many messages of hope.

We are very precious to God.

Heaven rules! Forever!

Our prayers do matter.

God rescues and saves His people.

Even in the hardest times, God is working His plan for His people.

And He can be trusted to keep His covenant with us.

These are truths, brothers and sisters, truths of the eternal life we now have. And to keep our footing sure as we go forward into the future, we need to stand firmly on the truths of God's reality.

The opening verse from Colossians is part of a

longer passage where Paul outlines our stories, yours and mine. We were once far away from God, separated from Him. Yet Christ's death made our peace with God, and He has brought us into His presence and declared us "holy and blameless as you stand before him without a single fault" (Colossians 1:22).

Your first thought might be, *But that's not me. I have many faults. I am not blameless.*

God declares, *Yes, you are!*

That is His truth, the reality He has brought about for His children. And as verse 23 states, we must plant our feet firmly in this reality. It changes our lives. If I cannot hold tightly to the belief that this is now my standing with God, if I cannot accept this or am always questioning whether or not I am "good enough" for God, then I am cheating myself of all that God wants to give me. If I can't believe this promise, then I'm probably also finding it difficult to believe and live out all of God's other promises.

If we are not building our lives on God's reality—*all* of His truth—we're building on shaky foundations that will not hold up as we go through life. Jesus compared it to building a house on sand, a futile construction that crashes in the rain and floods. In contrast, the house built on bedrock will stand through all storms.

We must build on the bedrock of God's truth. We must.

And if we feel our knees are shaky and our stance in God's reality is not firm, He always hears and answers the prayer of *Spirit, help my unbelief!*

MORE: Psalm 125:1, 2; Matthew 7:24-27; Ephesians 6:14

✒ UNTIL THE END! ✒

So be truly glad. There is wonderful joy ahead, even though you have to endure many trials for a little while.

– 1 PETER 1:6 –

If we turn to the very last verse in Daniel and read only that one verse, we'll lose some of its power. But when we read of all Daniel's experiences—his unshakeable trust in God and the terrifying visions of what is to come—and then finish with the last verse, we find that it will speak peace to our own souls.

You'll remember that Daniel was quite distressed by the visions of the future. They made him physically ill. For several days, he was in bed and had to take time off from his job. We can also become fretful and fearful as we read of the times still to come before Christ finally rules a kingdom of justice and peace. Even without reading those prophetic passages, all we need to do is look at the worrisome condition of the world today.

Daniel felt just as we do, and probably even more so—he had actually seen some of the future. So when the messenger from heaven speaks these words to Daniel, I feel a peace settling into my own soul, too:

> As for you, go your way until the end. You will rest, and then at the end of the days, you will rise again to receive the inheritance set aside for you. (Daniel 12:13)

We know our ultimate destination, brothers and sisters. We know the One who is in control of it all. We know His plan and what He's promised. Our times are in His hands.

As for us, let us continue to go forward, over the bridges of hope He's laid out for us in this journey. Finish the race, holding on to our hope. Then rest. Rise. And inherit!

MORE: Hebrews 3:14; 2 Corinthians 4:16; Hebrews 10:35, 36; Revelation 21:7

PRAYER TO STAY ON THE PATH:

Teach me how to live, O LORD. Lead me

along the right path.

- PSALM 27:11 -

WE'RE ON A MISSION

🌿 NOTHING, UNLESS... 🌿

This is why we work hard and continue to struggle...

- 1 TIMOTHY 4:10 -

We've just followed Daniel through both anxiety and hope. We can identify with him, and we can anchor our hope to many promises in that book.

Before we go on, take a moment to read the Psalm prayer for this chapter. Make it your own. Ask the Spirit to give you a clear perception of the path He wants you to take tomorrow and the next tomorrow.

Now let's move from the Old Testament to the New, from Daniel to the apostle Paul. Here's one interesting paragraph about Paul's life. He is traveling, but he stops to have a hurried meeting with the elders of the church in Ephesus. He tells them:

> And now I am bound by the Spirit to go to Jerusalem. I don't know what awaits me, except that the Holy Spirit tells me in city after city that jail and suffering lie ahead. But my life is worth nothing to me unless I use it for finishing the work assigned me by the Lord Jesus—the work of telling others the Good News about the wonderful grace of God. (Acts 20:22-24)

What phrases struck you?

Perhaps you were jarred by *I don't know what awaits me...* That can be an uneasy question for each of us every day, right?

Or did you catch your breath when you read that Paul had a specific word from the Spirit that suffering and jail were ahead? What would be your response if you had such a clear vision of your future?

Could it be that something about verse 24 sounded a call and lit a flame within you? Do you, too, declare that "My life is worth nothing unless I use it for the work assigned me by the Lord Jesus"?

In the last chapter, we looked at ways we can stand and remain strong. But *why* do we want to run the race well? Why do we, as Paul wrote in his letter to Timothy, work hard and continue to struggle? Why won't we give up? What makes our lives *worth something?*

Yes, we have been promised rewards. But rewards are not the only reason we must stay strong and courageous. We will keep going, enduring, and finishing the race because of who we are and whose we are and what we are to be. Adopted into God's family, we've been given a new identity and a new purpose in life.

Paul's speech tells us that he knew he had work assigned to him, and he was determined to do it. We, too, have been given a mission, brothers and sisters. That's why we will not give up.

MORE: *Philippians 3:12-14;1 Timothy 6:12; 2 Timothy 4:7*

 **BECAUSE OF WHO WE ARE**

Once you had no identity as a people; now you are God's people.
- 1 PETER 2:10 -

Our mission—our purpose—here on earth arises out of who we are.

How would you define your identity? Is it dependent on your career or your position in a company? Is it described by your role in your family life at this time? Is your identity tied to a social marker or a financial yardstick?

If your automatic response is that you're "just a nobody," know this: That's a lie of the enemy, designed to cheat you out of the life God offers anyone who comes to Him.

Your position, role, status, and circumstances in this world change constantly over the span of a lifetime. Either slow, subtle changes will come, or storms will devastate and shred your identity if it's hooked to anything in the temporal world. Think about what happens when a man's identity is anchored to his job, and he either retires or is, in one moment, fired. What happens when you've wrapped up your identity in your family and natural changes come—growth, marriage, death? What does a person do if they have based their identity on their tireless work for a cause and that cause suddenly collapses and ceases to exist?

Nothing in the temporal world defines your true identity. All these things are gone eventually. Only God's eternal definition of your identity will remain constant.

Do you know who you are, child of God? Scripture tells every believer that "once you had no identity as a people; now you are God's people." You have been given an identity that goes far beyond any earthly outline and designation.

If you haven't already, read the opening verse from Peter's letter to believers.

Those words were not written for early believers alone. Peter begins both his letters explaining that he's writing to all God's people who share a faith in Jesus Christ. So we take these as God's words to us, also.

The Scriptures use many phrases to describe God's people. Read this sampling, and know that this is who *you* are:

- His own special treasure (Exodus 19:5)

- Children and heirs of God (Galatians 3:26)

- Chosen and called by God (Ephesians 4:1)

- Purchased to be His own (Titus 2:14)

- God's very own possession (1 Peter 2:9)

- People who have received God's mercy (1 Peter 2:10)

- God's people (1 Peter 2:10)

Our stories are found early in the Bible, in Deuteronomy 4:20: "Remember that the LORD rescued you from the iron-smelting furnace of Egypt in order to make you his very own people and his special possession, which is what you are today." We, too, were rescued so that God could make us His very own people. God has taken the initiative to offer us a new identity, an identity that does not change or evaporate with shifts in worldly circumstances.

You may object to my application of Old Testament words to our lives today. You may think those words were only for the ancient Israelites.

But they were meant for us, too.

Jesus' assignment to Saul—later to be called Paul, the apostle—was that he was to spread the message that anyone who turned "from darkness to light, and from the power of Satan to God" and had faith in Jesus Christ would be forgiven and would become one of God's people (Acts 26:17, 18). Jesus opened the door for everyone.

So if you've turned to God and have faith in Christ, then you have a place as one of God's own people, and God's words to His people in ancient days are still His words to His people in "modern" days. He is the eternal God, not limited or changed by earthly divisions of time.

What you read in Scripture about God's people is true of your identity now. You are not a nobody, nor are you limited by who and what the world says you are. The eternal God has said you are one of His people, rescued to belong to Him.

MORE: Deuteronomy 7:6; Galatians 3:14, 29; Ephesians 3:6; Titus 2:14

⋙ GOD'S HOLY NATION ⋘

To all of you... who are loved by God and are called to be his own holy people. May God our Father and the Lord Jesus Christ give you grace and peace.

– **ROMANS 1:7** –

There's a word I avoided in the last meditation. You may have noticed. I purposely did not list it among the others because I didn't want to scare you off.

Because, you know, the word *holy* does scare some people. It's been used in derogatory ways that make us cringe. It implies a standard that we know is impossible to achieve, and so we would like to hide from the light that shows us how un-holy we are.

And I firmly believe that this gut-level reaction we might have to "being holy" is a deception by the enemy of our souls. He's hijacked the word and twisted its connotations and emotional impact. He wants us to react negatively to holiness!

But know this, sisters and brothers: God has called us to be His holy people.

Let's look at two important words in that last sentence: *called* and *holy.*

First of all, what does it mean to be called by God?

The original Greek word that is usually translated as *called* is *klēsis.*

According to the "NLT Word Study System" in Tyndale Publishers' New Living Translation

Bible, this word means "an invitation to someone to accept responsibilities for a particular task or a new relationship. God calls/invites the believer to relationship with him or to a particular role in his Kingdom."

Does this add an extra layer of meaning for you when you read phrases like *called by God, called to belong to Christ, called by God for a certain work?* God has put out the invitation.

Then let's look at the word *holy*. Again, Tyndale gives added insight. In Scripture, the word is used in three ways. It can mean:

- Standing apart from sin and evil

- Consecrated or set aside for sacred use

- Characteristic of God

Did you notice that these definitions of *holy* are not a measure of perfection? They are, instead, a matter of identity, character, and purpose.

Shall we let go of our thoughts about our flaws, our shortcomings, and our inability to measure up to the yardstick of perfection? God's Word to us is that Jesus is the one who is making us perfect. Yup, He is my Champion! I'm depending on Him to do that.

I struggled for a long time to make myself perfect. That didn't go so well. Then I discovered the reality: It is Jesus in me who is doing the perfecting. What a change that made in my life! And because that was such a struggle for me for many years of my life, I would like to share more of God's Word on this. If you are chained (as I was) by the idea that you've got to make yourself perfect, please ask for the Spirit's help and then dig into the MORE Scriptures below. I know I've listed more than usual, but I needed to be told by my Father, over and over, that I must let go of the "yardstick." So here are His words to you. We are called to belong to God, to be His people. Jesus is the only one who can make us perfect.

(By the way, you'll see many of those Scriptures in the letters to the Corinthians. I find that interesting—if there was any church that was far from perfect, it was the church at Corinth. They had many serious problems. Yet they, like us, were called to be holy. And one more thing I can't help but point out—Jesus is not ashamed to call us His brothers and sisters!)

Let's lay aside the idea of "perfect" and concentrate on these three definitions of *holy* as we find out what it means to be called to be God's holy people.

MORE: 1 Corinthians 1:2, 30; 1 Corinthians 6:11; Ephesians 5:25, 26; Philippians 1:11; Colossians 1:21, 22; Hebrews 2:11; Hebrews 10:10, 14; Hebrews 12:2

 LIVING AS CITIZENS OF HEAVEN

Therefore I... beg you to lead a life worthy of your calling,
for you have been called by God.

- EPHESIANS 4:1 -

We were driving through an unfamiliar town, looking for highway signs, not quite sure where our next turn would be. To complicate matters, a popular county fair was in full swing in the community, and long lines of traffic crept through the streets. A distance that we could probably have covered in ten minutes took us *forever.* (That might be a slight exaggeration.)

At one intersection, a policeman was directing traffic. I hesitated for just a moment, not sure if I wanted to go straight or turn right. That was one moment too long for him. His gestures and facial expression relayed his impatience and aggravation at this out-of-stater who was slowing his traffic flow.

I've probably traveled through that town only two or three times—but this is the memory I have whenever the name of that municipality is mentioned. And while I know that my feelings about that brief incident should not color my thoughts about the citizens in that town... well, my emotional reaction still focuses on that less-than-welcoming introduction.

I wonder how many encounters we might have—brief or lengthy—that leave someone with definite feelings or ideas about citizens of heaven, God's holy nation.

When Peter wrote his two letters to early Christians, he used some of the same words God had used when He spoke to the Israelites in the Sinai desert. God had rescued the descendants of Jacob from slavery in Egypt, and He was choosing their nation to be His special people. They were His royal priests, a holy nation, and His own special possession. They, among all the people on earth, were to be used for God's purposes, to exhibit God's way of living to the rest of the world, and to show what it meant to be God's people. At least a thousand years later, Peter used the same words when writing to believers.

What does it mean for us to be a "holy nation"?

Let's consider the first meaning of *holy:* Standing apart from sin and evil. As Paul wrote to the Ephesians (in the opening verse), we're to live a life worthy of our calling to be God's people. Some of the writers of the New Testament letters put it another way: "Remember that we are citizens of another kingdom. Live as citizens of that kingdom."

We've been moved to Christ's kingdom, and we're already living there. As we step into the future every day, constantly moving toward the time when Christ will set up His kingdom here, our attitudes and behavior will surely be affected by our identity as citizens of Christ's kingdom. God's Word gives us guidelines on how citizens of God's holy nation will act. Many specific actions and attitudes are addressed in Scripture, but these words from Titus give us a good summary:

> For the grace of God has been revealed, bringing salvation to all people. And we are instructed to turn from godless living and sinful pleasures. We should live in this evil world with wisdom, righteousness, and devotion to God, while we look forward with hope to that wonderful day when the glory of our great God and Savior, Jesus Christ, will be revealed. He gave his life to free us from every kind of sin, to cleanse us, and to make us his very own people, totally committed to doing good deeds. (Titus 2:11-14)

There's much to ponder in these few verses. We no longer live "godless" lives—because we are not godless!

Our allegiance now belongs to God's kingdom, and His kingdom operates on different principles than does the kingdom of this world. We live as His holy nation right where we are today, standing apart from sin and evil, living with wisdom, righteousness, and devotion to our God. That is what we are called to do. It's also interesting to note that this is God's plan since before the beginning of time—that His people live according to His direction, even while temporarily in Satan's territory. We live as "aliens" during our journey on this earth. (See Ephesians 2:10 and 2 Timothy 1:9)

And, you notice, here again we read that Christ is the one who cleanses us and makes us perfect— we'll never accomplish that ourselves. He's our Champion! He'll take care of the completion and perfection of His people.

Our job? Be committed to living as God's people, citizens of heaven.

MORE: Philippians 3:20; Colossians 3:12-14; 1 Thessalonians 4:7, 8

 TEMPLE OF GOD

And you are living stones that God is building into his spiritual temple.

- **1 PETER 2:5** -

Until I learned that *holy* does not mean *living perfectly,* I was often confused when I read about the Tabernacle and the Temple in the Old Testament. How could bowls and censers and bread and sacrifices be holy? Then this was explained: *Holy* can mean "consecrated or set aside for sacred use," and I began to understand.

Did you know that because you belong to Jesus, God has not only called you to live like His holy people but also to be consecrated for His sacred use? As we go forward into the future, there is one thing of which we can be certain: God will use His holy people to accomplish His plans and purposes—plans that have existed before the beginning of the world.

Are you beginning to get a sense of how we fit into God's ongoing work?

God's holy people are to be His Temple here on earth.

We talked earlier about God living with His people. The Jews understood that the physical temples they built represented God's presence among them. It was where God lived, where they went to meet God.

Now, God says, *we* are His Temple. His presence on earth resides with His people, and His visible presence will be there. Built together as a temple for Himself, we are to be the place where God is alive and working, and the place where anyone can go to see and meet Him.

How's that for a big assignment for your life here on earth? Your life is not just a flimsy wisp of smoke that drifts away and serves no purpose. Your life is a stone in what God is building on earth today—one more piece of evidence that God is alive and He is here among us.

This is another reason we cannot give up. We

go on, into the future of tomorrow and as many tomorrows as we're given, through whatever we will meet on our individual paths, knowing that we have been chosen and purposed for God's sacred use—as a living witness to His presence here on earth.

What do people see when they meet us? Do they know God lives with you and me? Perhaps they will not identify God's presence at first, but can they see something different in our lives than in what they see everywhere else in the world?

Does our world—and I'm talking only about the small sphere that each of us inhabits—does our world know that God lives here?

MORE: 1 Corinthians 6:19; 1 Corinthians 3:16; Ephesians 2:19-22;
Hebrews 3:6

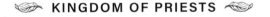 KINGDOM OF PRIESTS

What's more, you are his holy priests
- **1 PETER 2:5** -

Peter has yet one more key to our identity and mission as God's holy people. Besides being built as God's spiritual temple, we are His holy priests.

For many years, this puzzled me. My religious background knew nothing of priests. Actually, I don't think I spent much time or energy puzzling over it—I just skimmed over those references and did not realize they could apply to me.

I missed so much for so many years.

Do you ever feel as though your life is just "ho-hum"? As though God really hasn't given you anything special to do? Or if He truly has given you a gift, you don't even know what it might be? Do you sometimes think that your being Jesus' disciple doesn't make much of a difference to anyone else?

Here's your special privilege of service: You are one of God's holy priests.

The references to being God's priests took on great meaning for me once I paid attention to what I was reading in the Old Testament. Here I found clues that add to my identity while I'm still living on this earth. Numbers 18:7 tells us that God considered the priesthood a "special privilege of service." So when we, God's holy people today, are told that we are also His priests, it is a special privilege of service for us.

Of course, these Scriptures do not mean we have to actually enter the priesthood. Just as God is building us into a *spiritual* temple, our role as priests of our God has more to do with our purpose and mission in life.

When God first established the position of priests in the tabernacle, they were given three responsibilities: to carry the Ark of the Covenant, the box that contained God's law and represented His presence; to serve the Lord; and to pronounce blessings in His name. (See Deuteronomy 10:8)

We are given the same responsibilities:

To "carry" God's presence and His Word. We've just looked at passages that tell us we are the temple of God here on earth. We carry His presence and His Word with us. His Spirit dwells here with us. A verse from Malachi tells us that priests were to give people the truth of God's Word and live in awe and reverence of Him. They were to instruct people and be God's messengers. (See Malachi 2:5-7) God's holy priests today live in God's presence and carry His Word and His truth.

To serve our Lord. "Serving the Lord" is a phrase often used in Christian conversation. What does it mean?

We immediately see the connection to *servant.* A servant, according to Merriam-Webster, is someone who performs duties for another, either as a worker or a worshipper. Aren't we both? We work as God's representatives here, carrying on His mission, and we also serve Him because we worship the Almighty.

Now, do we have to be involved in some kind of special missions or ministry? Not necessarily, but His will becomes our will. That's serving the Lord.

If we follow our own will, we are not serving Him. Jesus reminded us that no one can serve two masters (Matthew 6:24).

A begrudging bending to His commands is not what He desires, either. He desires "serving with gladness, coming into His presence with singing and joy" (Psalm 100:2 AP). This is part of the mission of God's people; to carry out His will and do so with joy, enthusiasm, and thankfulness for His blessings.

As His representative, to bless others. God's holy nation of Israel was to be a blessing to the entire earth. So are we. We're to bring God's light and goodness into every mile of our journey here. The ultimate blessing is doing good to our enemies instead of repaying evil for evil. We are told in 1 Peter 3:9 not to retaliate to insults. "Instead, pay them back with a blessing. That is what God has called you to do, and he will grant you His blessing."

If you're looking for instructions for your role as God's priest, you'll find more guidance in the Scriptures. We're to worship and praise, dress ourselves in godliness, and offer our sacrifices.

Wait. Offer sacrifices? Like the ancient priests did? Grain and goats and birds and bulls? Reading all the lists of sacrifices the priests offered in the Old Testament can almost put you to sleep. A continual procession of offerings came to the altar, and all of them had to be killed or sacrificed in specific ways.

Our sacrifices (thankfully) are of a different kind. But they, too, are to be continual. Here's a list:

- A broken, repentant heart (Psalm 51:16, 17)

- Showing love and seeking to know the Lord (Hosea 6:6)

- Thankfulness (Psalm 50:14, 23)

- Doing what is good, loving mercy, walking humbly before God (Micah 6:8 and Hebrews 13:16)

- Continual praise (Hebrews 13:15)

- Proclaiming our allegiance to Him (Hebrews 13:15)

- Sharing with those in need (Hebrews 13:16 and Philippians 4:18)

- Giving our bodies—every part of who we are—to God for his service (Romans 12:1)

God has given us this privilege of serving Him in all these ways. It's a big job! Whatever roads we walk in the future, we are walking as priests of the eternal King.

MORE: 1 Chronicles 16:4; Malachi 2:5-7; Romans 12:11; Revelation 1:6

CHILDREN OF THE MOST HIGH

As a result, you can show others the goodness of God, for
he called you out of the darkness into his wonderful light.

– 1 PETER 2:9 –

There is one more definition of *holy:* "characteristic of God."

We are God's holy people, His holy nation, and His holy and royal priests because we are children of the Most High King. Jesus even calls us His brothers and sisters. We are part of the family of God.

How did we get here? It is an amazing story, isn't it? The God Who Makes All Things New gifted us with new lives. And because our new lives were birthed and are sustained by the Spirit of God, we should certainly be showing a family resemblance to our Father and Brother.

That might seem like a self-important thing to claim. It's one thing for us to say we are citizens of the Kingdom of Heaven. But if we talk of having the character of God—that's rather bold, isn't it?

But this is what the Scriptures tell us: The new nature God brought to life in you is created to be like Him—truly righteous and holy! (See Ephesians 4:24) This new life was created to bear the characteristics of our heavenly Father.

This is how we walk into the future, sisters and brothers—we walk as children of the Most High

King. Not yet perfectly exhibiting His character, but growing up into it. Learning from Him and living accordingly.

Why is this identity important as we face the future? Because we are meant to live like sons and daughters of the King. God's plan is that through us, the world will see who He is and what He does.

At a social gathering, a woman approached me. She seemed familiar, yet I could not recall her name. "You're Doris's daughter?" she asked.

Now, that's a question I haven't been asked in decades. My mom left this earth and went on to her new life almost twenty-eight years ago.

The woman told me who she was, and then I remembered—she and Mom had worked together for many years at one of the local schools.

"I'm seeing more and more of Mom these days when I look in the mirror," I answered. I do think I'm looking more like Mom than at any other time in my life.

The woman smiled. "That's not a bad thing," she said. It warmed my heart to know that she had good memories of who my mother was.

Do I look like my heavenly Father? Do people know I am His daughter by observing how I talk and act? Am I showing more and more family resemblance to my Brother?

We show others who our Father is by how we

treat them. Jesus repeated this throughout His teachings—be true children of your Father! Act like Him! "You must be compassionate, just as your Father is compassionate" (Luke 6:36). "And be kind to your enemies. Be good to them. Then you'll be acting like a true child of your Father, because He is kind to the unthankful and wicked. And you'll be rewarded for it!" (Luke 6:35 AP).

Paul wrote to the Ephesians, "Be kind to each other and forgive each other, just like Christ forgives you" (Ephesians 4:32 AP). As a matter of fact, we're to imitate God in everything we do. Everything we do should show others the goodness of our Father.

There's another way we can make God's goodness known: We can tell the story of our own rescue.

I've mentioned Psalm 107 several times. It's a chapter full of stories about people who've been rescued by God. The psalm begins with this: "Give thanks to the Lord. He is so good. His love never quits. Have you been rescued by Him? Then speak up, and tell your story!" (my paraphrase).

We children of the Most High can show the goodness of God by telling others how we were rescued from darkness and famine, brought to the palace, and given a new life as an heir of the King.

My story is also outlined in Psalm 116: The Lord "saved me from death, my eyes from tears, my feet from stumbling. And so I walk in the LORD's presence as I live here on earth!" (Psalm 116:8, 9) What better illustration of God's kindness and compassion than this rescue that I know first-hand?

No matter what tomorrow brings, I desire to stand as a testament to the goodness of God—by treating others in ways that show whose daughter I am; by showing all that God has done and is doing in my life; and by my gratefulness and praise to Him.

MORE: Matthew 5:14, 16; Philippians 1:11; Philippians 2:14, 15; Ephesians 5:8, 9; Colossians 3:10

✺ ENTRUSTED WITH A MISSION ✺

Just as you sent me into the world, I am sending them into the world... I am praying not only for these disciples but also for all who will ever believe in me through their message.
- **JOHN 17:18, 20 (JESUS, PRAYING)** -

Let's imagine, for a moment. You are working at your desk, at a good, quiet, secure job with many benefits. You're quite content there.

Then the owner of the company calls you into his office, and he has shocking news.

"I'm going to send you out on the road. We want you to get out there and convince folks to sign on for our new program. Let them know it's the best plan they'll ever have the opportunity to participate in. We know it will be difficult. You'll have a lot of opposition and competition. Your life may even be in danger. But I'm handing this job over to you."

"But..." Your mind quickly calls up all kinds of objections. You don't even know all the details of this new program. You've never done anything like this before. Why you? You're not the best guy for the job. Oh—and that part about your life being in danger? You aren't sure you want to sign up for that.

Do you recognize this scenario?

Jesus did this just before He left this world. He turned the mission over to His disciples of every era—and that would include you and me.

He came, in the first place, on a mission to bring people back to God. While He was here, He broke all the barriers between God and us, but there is still much work to be done in rebuilding the relationship to our Creator. And as long as God gives people time to turn around and come back to Him, Jesus' disciples carry on with the mission given to us by our King.

We are part of God's plan being worked out here on earth. Everyone has been given a role in the mission and equipped with abilities that will make them effective in that role. Sometimes we seem to be living common, ordinary lives, and we might think we are not obeying Jesus' Great Commission to go and make disciples of all nations. But every life, no matter how "ordinary," touches other lives. And Paul wrote that "nothing you do for the Lord is ever useless" (1 Corinthians 15:58). Whether it's living in Hong Kong as missionaries for forty years, or cooking meals at the local elementary, or daily interceding for others in the privacy of your own home, or showing kindness, or encouraging others, or giving generously, your life is part of the mission of bringing people back to God.

So as we face tomorrow, we go forward knowing that we have been entrusted with Jesus' mission. God created us anew to make us His children, His people, His holy nation, His temple, and His priests here on earth. He's had plans since before He created us, and we are an integral part of how He is working out His plans in this world.

I am reminded of the Isaiah 53 prophecy that God's good plan would prosper in the hands of the Messiah. And now the Messiah has entrusted us with the mission!

We could feel overwhelmed by that. Except for one thing.

The opening illustration fails at the endpoint. In our imaginary scene, the boss sends you out on the mission, trembling, apprehensive, uncertain— overwhelmed. But the reality of our mission is quite different. We are being sent out by the King who has all authority in heaven and earth, and our hope knows we have His promise: "I'm going with you. And you will have my power."

MORE: Matthew 28:18-20; Acts 1:8; 2 Corinthians 5:17-20; Colossians 3:16, 17; Jude 1:3

 **BRING GLORY TO GOD**

Come, let us tell of the LORD's greatness.
- **PSALM 34:3** -

Have you ever tried to imagine the apostle Paul, sitting down to write a letter to the believers in the city of Corinth? It was a wicked, pagan city, and the new church there was not living in a protective bubble. Many of the converts to Christianity were struggling with influences, habits, philosophies, and customs from their old lives. Paul kept in touch, and as he sat down to write, he may have been wondering just where to begin addressing all the problems.

(However—I must insert this, even though it's off topic—in the letters to the Corinthians we find some of the most hope-full lines in Scripture. Just browse through the pages. Paul declares that these believers have been called by God to be His holy people. They've been given spiritual gifts to keep them strong, they've been invited into partnership with Jesus, and Christ has made them right with God [pure, holy, and free from sin]. Paul goes on and on about all the hope God has given us. And all this was written to the Corinthian church, which was plagued by so many problems. No one is a lost cause, my friend! God's hope is for all of us, no matter where we are in our growing up as God's children.)

Okay, back to Paul's letters to the new believers in Corinth. He addressed some of the questions and issues creating divisions among them. In the middle of a discussion about whether or not those who had become Christians should or should not follow a particular practice, Paul wrote, "Well, whatever you do, be sure you're doing everything to bring God honor and glory" (1 Corinthians 10:31 AP).

That verse was probably one of the first Bible verses I was given to memorize as a child. You, too? We were taught to always act in ways that honored and glorified God.

Honor and glorify God. Christians might use that phrase often, but exactly what does it mean? How do we glorify God? How do we bring Him glory? Isn't He already a glorious, majestic, almighty God?

Let's begin to tackle those questions by looking at our human interactions. If we honor someone, we recognize their character, achievements, or actions as outstanding, beyond the average, and worthy of notice. Similarly, when we give someone the glory, we are giving them all the credit. They're deserving of praise and accolades and admiration. (Or, in contrast, we accuse someone of "grabbing all the glory," which means we're usually disgusted because they've taken far too much credit and praise when they do not deserve it.)

My friend Rebecca has put *glorifying God* into today's language. She simply calls it, "Making God famous."

Yes! Our God is already a glorious, majestic, and almighty God. These aspects of who He is will never be added to or diminished by anything we say or do. That's one type of glory.

But when we *give God glory and honor,* we acknowledge who He is and what He does. We talk about His greatness. We relate the wonderful things He's done. We celebrate Him. We give Him our applause and adoration. We make Him famous.

MORE: Psalm 99:3; Isaiah 43:7; 2 Thessalonians 1:12

 MAKING HIM FAMOUS

All honor and glory to God forever and ever!
He is the eternal King, the unseen one who
never dies; he alone is God. Amen.
— **1 TIMOTHY 1:17** —

If we're wondering how to glorify God—how it would look in our lives—we have good models. Many of the psalms were written specifically to praise and honor God. Their purpose was to make Him famous!

Psalm 145 is an excellent example. It begins with the statement that no one can measure God's greatness and then goes on to sing praises of this God who deserves all the credit. "Everyone will share the story of your wonderful goodness" (verse 7) and "Your faithful followers will praise you" (verse 10) challenge me to speak up more often and give God all the credit for what He has done.

Psalm 107, that chapter listing the accounts of so many rescues, repeats after each, "Let them praise the LORD for his great love and the wonderful things he has done." As I've said before, many of us will find our stories there. Let us give God all the glory for our rescue!

Psalm 71 is amazing. Sometime when you have a few quiet moments, sit down and read it slowly, entering into the feeling and backstory of each section. Here's a quick outline:

Verses 1-4. The writer is in trouble. His

adversaries are powerful. He needs God's protection and help.

Verses 5-8. He declares that his only hope is God. He's trusted God, and God has been with him for a lifetime. Others have seen God's strength and protection in his life. "No wonder I am always praising you! I can't stop!" (v. 8, AP)

Verses 9-11. Now he is old, his strength is failing, and his enemies are plotting his death.

Verses 12-13. He prays for help once more.

Verses 14-16. And he keeps on hoping. And praising. "I will tell everyone about you and what you've done." (v. 15 & 16, AP)

Verses 17-19. He's spent a lifetime telling others about the wonderful things God has done, and now that he's old and gray, "Let me proclaim your power to this new generation, your mighty miracles to all who come after me." (v. 18)

Verses 20-24. He is, right now, suffering much hardship. But he knows God will comfort and restore him again. It has not happened yet, but he is already *looking forward* to another chance to talk about how wonderful God has been.

I hope I didn't rush that too much. Did you catch the power of this? He's an old man whose health is failing, who knows people are plotting against him, who is suffering—and yet his focus is always on giving God the glory for all the wonderful things He has done throughout the years.

God gets all the glory. We assume the psalm was written by David, a king we think was one of the great heroes of the Bible. But David points our admiration to God, the one who gets all the credit and all the praise.

We have the same purpose—to glorify God. We can do it just as David did, through everything we say. The account of my rescue (salvation) is certainly a cause for giving God the glory—only He could save me. The miracles He's done in our lives call for praise, and He has done miracles for every one of us. Watch for them; they aren't always big, thunderous, flashy events, but I'm a firm believer that God sends gifts of His love into our lives every day, some of which are truly supernatural. And speaking of everyday gifts, try to list all the wonderful things for which you're thankful today. Right now. All good things are from God, even joy in the hearts of those who don't believe in Him. (Acts 14:17)

Do we sometimes try to grab the credit ourselves? I know I do, but I'm trying to change that because everything I have, God has given me and made happen. He gets the credit, not me.

Besides our *telling*, we also bring Him glory by:

- How we live, especially among our unbelieving neighbors (1 Peter 2:12, Matthew 5:16)

- Using our talents infused by His strength and His energy to serve others (1 Peter 4:10, 11)

- *All* the results of our living as Christ's disciples (John 15:8, Philippians 1:9-11)

I realized this chapter was getting long, and I'd planned that this last meditation would be the shortest, but you know what? When we start talking of the Lord's greatness, it's difficult to draw things to a close.

So let's never make an end of it. Let's travel down whatever roads are ahead and make God famous as we go. It's the ultimate purpose and mission of His children.

Who can list the glorious miracles of the LORD?
Who can ever praise him enough?
(Psalm 106:2)

MORE: Psalm 145:10-12; Jude 1:24, 25; Revelation 1:5, 6

PRAYER TO KEEP PERSPECTIVE:

LORD, remind me how brief my time on earth will be... how fleeting my life is.

- **PSALM 39:4** -

WE HAVE MORE
LIFE COMING

✎ A GLIMPSE OF LIFE ✎

They saw it all from a distance and welcomed it.

- HEBREWS 11:13 -

I caught a glimpse.

After days of clouds and rain, the sky beamed blue as white puffs drifted by, and the sun unleashed brilliance. At four in the afternoon, I was running errands: a drop at the bank, dash into the library, check the post office, hurry to an appointment.

But before I got into my car, something brought me to a halt and told me to take note: Look how far the shadows stretch, how low the sun hangs over the western hills, and how the November cold has seeped into our town in spite of the sun.

This moment came at the end of a day when...

... I read the obituary of a prominent man from our area whose life-long influence in both church and business helped to shape this community, its culture, and its economy. He died last week. The obituary read, "He went to see His Lord."

... My youngest grandson came to my door, carefully holding something and wearing a gleeful grin. "Grandma, I have a present for you." He presented me with copies of their most recent family portraits. Beautiful, each one of them, all spruced up and smiling. But when did this happen? When did Oldest Grandson grow so tall? When did Granddaughter turn into such a lady? Why is the youngest no longer our baby?

... Sister called. We were trying to get something on our family schedule. First available day was December 1. December? What had happened to November? For that matter, I didn't think I was quite finished with October yet.

The moment of blue coldness in late afternoon whispered of winter, the year, and time slipping away, and—how do I describe what happened?

I only know these moments as *glimpses*. That's what I've named them. The Spirit permits me a peek through a window in the universe. Or maybe, for a few seconds, He puts God-dimension glasses over my eyes.

Whatever it was that happened, I considered it a gift. I'd been asking God for a better understanding of this:

His government and its peace will never end. He will rule with fairness and justice from the throne of his ancestor David for all eternity. The passionate commitment of the LORD of Heaven's Armies will make this happen! (Isaiah 9:7)

Eternity and something that *will never end.* This is a hard thing to take hold of. Everything of this world begins and ends and is measured by the time between those events. We do not know how to live without that regulation.

That day, for just a breath, a blink, I glimpsed my life outside of time. My real life—your real life, child of God—is in a realm outside the measures by which we arrange our lives now. In that one glimpse, my kind Father gave me an assurance that my life goes far beyond the years that slip away so quickly.

You're familiar with Hebrews 11, that chapter full of accounts of people who lived by faith. The chapter includes several verses that used to trouble me. Verse 13 says that "all these people died... they did not receive what was promised..." and verse 39 repeats, "none of them received all that God had promised." Doesn't God do what He promises? Isn't that what our hope is built on, His truthfulness and dependability?

But we have to read the complete sentences: Verse 13 says, "But they saw it all from a distance and welcomed it." May I put five exclamation points after that? (My editor will frown.) They saw it from a distance and looked forward to it! They had that sight—the eyes of hope and faith—that saw life as greater than just the years between birth and death. God does keep all His promises, and some of them are fulfilled in that part of our lives beyond what we see and know now.

Ask God to give you a glimpse—no, ask for more than one glimpse—ask Him to fix your gaze on your life that does not end. It is a life He has planned for you, His treasured child.

MORE: 2 Corinthians 4:18; Hebrews 11:13-16

🌿 WAKING UP TO THE NEW 🌿

*For you have been born again, but not to a life that will
quickly end. Your new life will last forever because it comes
from the eternal, living word of God.*

— 1 PETER 1:23 —

I felt resurrected.

A friend and I spent two days on a long, hard drive to a new vacation spot. We arrived late on the second night. Driving into the lane of the rented cottage, we saw the house was completely dark, without a single light to help us find our way to the porch and the back door. We unloaded luggage by the headlights of the car, felt our way to light switches in the house, and made ourselves as comfortable as we could without much knowledge of our surroundings.

And we finally fell asleep.

The next morning, I awoke to a new world. It was a beautiful morning, with the waters of the bay shimmering under a clean blue and pink sky, in a place completely different from the rolling hill country I had left two days before. I recognized similarities to the world I had left—people living in dwellings, traveling along roads or paths, eating, working, playing—but life in this new place, I was about to discover, was quite different. Even the air felt different.

Will resurrection be something like that? After long, hard slogs, we fall asleep in the dark but then awaken to a bright new day, to things new and much different from anything we've previously known. And, certainly, beyond anything we have ever imagined. We will not know and understand that new place until we are there.

From this point forward in this book, I will often have a problem with finding the right words. We are now looking into a future of which we know very little, and we're going to try to grasp a reality we do not yet know.

Some will argue that the Bible has much to say about our lives in the eternal future. Yes, it does. The problem is, again, with words. What God has given us in Scripture concerning our future lives is given through prophecies and visions, utilizing much symbolism and imagery to convey ideas. What is coming is something unknown to our experience, and, I believe, much of our future cannot be described in the limited words we now use. So we must use the language that we do know, images and ideas that are familiar, in order to communicate. For example, the Bible talks of the four corners of the earth, but we do not interpret that to mean the world has literal corners and thus is flat. We know that it means "every part of the world." But when it comes to things we do *not* know, symbolism and metaphors can lead to differing interpretations or definitions. When prophecy says the lion and the lamb will lie down together—does this mean there will be lions and lambs in the new world? Or is it, instead, an image of the peace that Christ's rule will bring to the world?

So, I do not want to be dogmatic or debate things we do not know—at least, that *I* do not claim to understand. Indeed, Scripture says there are many things that are not for us to know and that even the prophets who delivered God's message did not always understand who the message was for or how events would come about. So I am not going to delve into prophecy about which-nation-will-do-what-and-when. We will not focus on timelines and national histories, but on the hope that Christians have, a hope that transcends all the details, no matter *what* we meet on the road through the future.

I am not bothered by the places in this book where I will have to type, "I do not know" or, "I can't comprehend this." A prophecy in Zechariah 14:7 speaks of a day that will seem to break the "laws" of light and darkness, day and night. It will be a day "known only to the LORD." Some translations express that as "only the Lord knows when it will happen," while others render it, "only the Lord knows how it will happen." What is clear is this: Only the

Lord knows! I believe this declaration applies to much of prophecy.

Instead of trying to pin down ambiguous details, let's celebrate what our hope *does* know: the firm assurances God has given us about what lies ahead for His children.

Remember that our hope is confidence that we *will* be given what is promised, that God *will* do what He has said. We can walk with the faith and perseverance modeled in Hebrews 11 because our hope can *see* what is coming. We live with great expectation!

So then, to go back to our opening thought on resurrection, how can I believe that dead bodies will come back to life?

Because Jesus said He will do it, and He said it is the will of God.

MORE: John 6:39, 40; 1 Corinthians 15:21, 22; Hebrews 11:1

 STICKING WITH THE PLAN

For we know that when this earthly tent we live in is taken down (that is, when we die and leave this earthly body), we will have a house in heaven, an eternal body made for us by God himself and not by human hands.

- 2 CORINTHIANS 5:1 -

Now, in this very first chapter on our ultimate future, I will begin with a subject *I can't comprehend.* As a matter of fact, I can't even imagine what I can't imagine.

When we "wake up" to the new, one of the things we'll be celebrating is new bodies. My mind doesn't know where to go with the idea of resurrected bodies, immortal and heavenly.

For all of our lives, we've dealt with these bodies we're living in. We've experienced all kinds of joys and all kinds of problems associated with our physical homes. The very word *body* seems to be so rooted in this world that we've started to associate body with the "bad" and unspiritual part of us—the part we look forward to leaving behind.

But God has told us plainly that we will have new bodies. It's part of a promise He has made that He is making all things new, and that includes our bodies.

Many of us can identify with the verse from 2 Corinthians 5 that says we groan and sigh, dealing with these earthly bodies. Yes, they make us groan many times (some of us more than others). But Paul wrote in the same chapter that our deepest sighing is not just to be rid of the limitations of our current bodies, but it is a longing for our new bodies, planned and promised long ago by the God of all hope.

Paul compares these bodies we now have to a temporary dwelling—a tent we're living in. One day, each of us will see our tent taken down. And then we'll move into a new house built for us by God himself. This new dwelling will not be anything transitory or hounded by death and decay.

It will be the permanent dwelling God has for each of His children.

It reminds me of the opening scenes of our history, as God fashioned the first bodies and then breathed life into them. Those first bodies were meant to live forever. They weren't dying from the moment they were created. But here we are now, with bodies descended from Adam and Eve and bearing the results of rebellion against God—decay and death.

God *does* care about our bodies. They were part of His original design for us. So He has amazing plans for those who come to Him through Christ. His plan is to create anew—He has already breathed His Spirit into us, giving us a new, heavenly life; and someday, our bodies will also be renewed and eternal.

Scriptures say that God has prepared us for this. It's interesting to read 2 Corinthians 5:5 in different translations:

- [God] has fashioned us for this very purpose (NIV)

- God himself has prepared us for this (NLT)

- He who has prepared us for this very thing (ESV)

- He who hath wrought us for the selfsame thing (KJV)

That "thing" referred to is that our mortal bodies will be swallowed up by the immortal. God's plan is still that we will live in bodies that will not die. A glorious hope!

This has always been God's plan, wrote Paul. Then, in the same verse, he assures us that we have God's guarantee this *will* happen: He has given us His Holy Spirit, and it is the Spirit already within us who will "give life to your mortal bodies" (Romans 8:11).

God planned for His children to have immortal bodies.

He's sticking with His plan.

I'm sure of it.

And I'm sticking with this hope.

MORE: Isaiah 26:19; Romans 8:23; 2 Corinthians 5:1-5

🍃 SEED PLANTED FOR THE 🍃
UNIMAGINABLE

For our dying bodies must be transformed into bodies that
will never die; our mortal bodies must be transformed into
immortal bodies.

- 1 CORINTHIANS 15:53 -

Our natural tendency is to wonder and want to know what's ahead. What will our new bodies be like? Will I still have this same shape? Will you still have curly hair? Will we recognize each other? What "age" will we be? And what will these bodies be doing? Working? Playing? Hugging? Needing rest and food? Will the person whose body now craves running find that heaven has marathons? Will I be able to enjoy every food I want and not have to think about pounds and cholesterol?

Jesus talks about people feasting in His kingdom. In several of His parables, people recognize each other in the next life. Biblical prophecies have many references to places and activities we know now— things like farming and vineyards, productive work, travel, worship, and governing leaders. In books, articles, commentaries, and sermons, you'll find all sorts of opinions about what our bodies and lives will be like in our future life.

But when it comes right down to it, the references to "bodies" carry so much of earthly description and implication that we are at a loss to know or even begin to imagine what our new bodies will be like.

That's okay. Our puzzlement is quite Scriptural.

There is one thing that we do know—the bodies we have now will be resurrected. Death will be undone, and our bodies will be alive with new capacities and a new kind of existence. Not done away with, but brought into something so new we can't imagine it.

Of course, here is another place where I must say, "I can't explain this." I don't know how it can happen. But God says it will.

As I write this, it's the season of pumpkins. At a pumpkin festival, one of the events was the official weigh-off of many huge orange orbs aspiring to be the champion. Folks plant a seed no bigger than a thumbnail, and that small sliver grows into something hundreds of times larger, and very different. The winner this year exceeded all previous records—1,727.5 pounds of orange pumpkin, almost the size of a VW Bug. Imagine that.

But if you had never seen a pumpkin before, even a small one, could you have imagined such an outcome when you watched as a small seed was buried in the dirt?

The apostle Paul uses this analogy in 1 Corinthians 15 when he writes about our new, heavenly bodies. What we put into the ground at the end of this life is only "a bare seed" of what will be. And then, just as God brings giant pumpkins from thin disks of seed, at the resurrection He will give us the bodies He wants us to have.

How can we even imagine what those will be? We don't have the words or the capacity to grasp it, because we have never seen heavenly bodies.

We are promised these things, though:

Our earthly bodies are planted in the ground when we die, but they will be raised to live forever.

Our bodies are buried in brokenness, but they will be raised in glory.

They are buried in weakness, but they will be raised in strength.

They are buried as natural human bodies, but they will be raised as spiritual bodies.

We're now earthly people. We will be heavenly people someday.

The bodies we have now cannot inherit the kingdom of God—dying bodies cannot inherit what will last forever. And so, "our dying bodies must be transformed into bodies that will never die." (All of that is in 1 Corinthians 15:42-54.)

Suits me.

Even if I don't know all the details, what we are told holds so much hope.

I'm pretty sure I'll be quite content and satisfied in my new body.

MORE: *1 Corinthians 15:54; Philippians 3:21*

CERTAINTY OF RESURRECTION

And this is what he promised us–eternal life.

- 1 JOHN 2:25 NIV -

Jesus knew He was within hours of being arrested. He wanted to go to one of His favorite retreats to pray and prepare. So on their way to the Mount of Olives, He continued to give His disciples last-minute instructions. Again, what He had to say dismayed them:

"Tonight, all of you will desert me... But after I have been raised from the dead, I will go ahead of you to Galilee and meet you there." (Matthew 26:31, 32)

Peter, of course, jumped in first with his protest. No, Peter would never desert Jesus. Why, he would even die with his friend if necessary. The others all chimed in. They'd be there, too, they vowed. Can you imagine the scene? All of them, with adrenalin levels high, nervous in the dark night, feeling the fear creep in. They didn't know what was going to happen, but Jesus knew, and He was giving them a dark picture—

Wait.

Did they not hear it?

Did they not hear the rest of what He had said?

"And after I have been raised from the dead, I'll meet you back home in Galilee."

None of the Gospel writers give us any

indication that the disciples immediately pounced on this hope that Jesus would somehow be alive again after He died. They were too focused and anxious about the next few hours. It seems that none of them remembered their appointment with Jesus until days later when rumors started circulating that Jesus was alive again, and then it occurred to them that He had said He would go to Galilee.

We might be quick to think, *How could they miss what Jesus was saying?* If a friend told me she was going to die soon, but then she'd meet me later at our favorite restaurant, I would certainly catch that!

Were the disciples too possessed by the threat of the next few hours? Or was it that they simply couldn't believe such a thing could happen? After all, this was not the usual way of things—dying, and then walking the earth again in a few days.

What about us? Jesus says, "For it is my Father's will that all who see his Son and believe in him should have eternal life. I will raise them up at the last day" (John 6:40). Do we believe Him? Or are we too caught up in worrying about the next few days to let this amazing hope have any effect on us?

Jesus often taught in parables, and prophecy is largely framed in symbolism and imagery. But this hope is trumpeted clearly throughout the Bible: The power of death has been broken by one man, Jesus Christ. He holds the keys to the grave. His resurrection was God's announcement that He had the power to give immortal life, and He would give it to anyone who trusted Him to do it. God doesn't want anyone to miss the offer of His gift.

This gift is not only for the future, but it is also a gift for today. It gives God's children freedom from the fear of dying. Even as we experience our earthly sadness and loss, we have the joy of knowing that physical death is the doorway through which we step into even more life.

This is God's ultimate Romans 8:28 triumph—that out of death, the God who loves us will bring life. In the face of Satan's most powerful weapon against us, God works His most miraculous promises. We see the theme throughout the Bible that life will come out of death: Dying to self unites us with God; Jesus' death gave us life forever; and even though our physical death is wrenching, our wonderful heavenly Father uses it to bring us to Himself, making it the most wonderful day of our lives.

Believing that He will give us what He promised has the power to change how we face the future and to give us strength to keep going—we journey onward with our sights fixed on the eternal tomorrow.

MORE: John 5:24-26; John 6:47; John 11:25; Romans 5:21; Romans 6:23

ALREADY ON THE ROAD TO OUR DESTINY

We have the Holy Spirit within us as a foretaste of future glory.

Although some of us might be ready to trade in our broken, weak, and dying bodies right now for strong, glorious, immortal ones, we will have to wait.

However, in His gracious plan, God chose to give us a start on our forever lives as soon as we believed in Jesus Christ.

For one thing, He planted His Spirit in us and said it's the "first installment" of everything He intends to give His children.

As we've noted before, the Spirit gives us a special connection to God. He is our guide and teacher. The amazing thing is that God is already at work. He's not waiting to make us "perfect someday."

As soon as we believe, God's Spirit comes to live in us. The Spirit births a new nature, "created to be like God" (Ephesians 4:24). Does that remind you of any other passage? Perhaps the first creation, when man was created in God's image and God breathed the breath of life into him?

We decided, instead, to go our own way, and look where that's taken us. But God offers us rescue from the mess we've made, and His plan is to restore the glory that we lost.

In this stained, tainted, sin-diseased me, God began a new life, created in His image! He is doing away with the old, giving birth to the new, and giving me His own life once again by breathing His Spirit into me. A new creation!

God has already begun the work of transforming us to be His children, exhibiting all the characteristics of His family. It's a process that will only be completed someday in the "age to come," but God has already begun. If this is the first installment, what all might He have planned for us?

We know it will be glorious. Paul wrote in Colossians that Christ living in us is the "hope of glory" or the "assurance of sharing his glory" (Colossians 1:27). Many of us came to Christ to escape eternal punishment, and Christ does save us from hell. But there is so much more for the children of God!

Some of that "so much more" is waiting for us in heaven. And some of it is already being showered upon us.

The Word tells us that, as God's children, we already have access to our Father's rich storehouses, both of His blessings and His resources. Every day of our journey here, we receive gifts of His love, and every day He says, "I am here to help you." He has given us individual gifts through His Spirit so that we can help, serve, and strengthen each other. He promises to supply whatever we need—and these promises do cover every aspect of life. As Peter wrote, living by the promises will enable us to share God's divine nature and escape the corruption of the world. That's a powerful promise.

Our hope knows that God is already in the process of giving *more life* to His people.

MORE: 2 Corinthians 3:16-18; Colossians 3:10; 2 Peter 1:3, 4

PRAYER TO KEEP UNATTACHED:

Turn my eyes from worthless things, and

give me life through your word.

- PSALM 119:37 -

"REJOICE FOREVER
IN MY CREATION"

THE CROWN OF LIFE

*God blesses those who patiently endure testing and
temptation. Afterward they will receive the crown of life
that God has promised to those who love him.*

- JAMES 1:12 -

As much as I like traveling, adventuring, and
exploring, the best part of all that is coming home.

Our small village stretches along a ridge and
spills down the hillsides. In this county of roads
that curve through the hills and valleys, one of
my favorite views is about three miles from home
when, from other heights on the highway, I catch

quick glimpses of our town. If I'm driving in the day, I can almost pick out my own home in the buildings outlined against the sky. The view is especially welcoming at night, when the lights crowning the hill shine out from the darkness and announce *home.*

We've spent a long time on this journey, thinking together about facing the future with hope. We've meditated on who we are and who travels with us; on staying strong and enduring; and on why we cannot quit. And where does all this lead us? Where is *home* for our journey?

I used to wonder why God doesn't tell us more. If heaven is such a desirable place, why use so much symbolism and figurative language, like a veil that keeps us from seeing clearly? Why not give us concrete details we can grab and hold on to?

He does give us an abundance of information. So much, in fact, that we can only touch a small part of it here. He does not describe in detail because we only understand the language of this world where we now live. What is coming will be so new it must be detailed in new words and ways—which we don't yet know. But God, in His love and kindness toward us, has given us enough that our hope can know. And as we travel, the darkness along this path only serves to make home shine brighter, like the shining jewels of a crown.

So, fellow pilgrim, here are some of the things our hope grabs and holds on to...

Take a moment to read the opening verse again.

So many words I'd like to emphasize: *blesses, patiently, afterward, promised.* But for now, think about *the crown of life.* (Take some time on your own to ponder the richness of the other words.)

The word *crown* immediately brings to mind a prize or award. The crown of life will be an honor bestowed. If the going is tough today—yes, and if it looks like things might get even tougher as you keep going into tomorrow—one thing our hope does know is that *afterward,* there will be rewards.

For me, this verse also carries another definition of *crown:* pinnacle, peak, highest point. The crown of life, the pinnacle of life. Life, in its highest, purest, fullest state; life, as the Creator intended to give His people who were made to be like Him. This is what we will be granted if we endure.

Here is another place I struggle to find words. How can we describe such a life when it is beyond anything we have known or can know in our earthly experience? When Jesus said He came to give people a full and abundant life, He meant both a rich life here on this earth and an even greater life in eternal realms.

In 1806, Thomas Kelly wrote the song, "Praise the Savior, ye who know Him," and found a phrase to describe this *crown of life:* "Things which are not now, nor could be, then shall be our own."

The apostle Paul used the phrase *the time of perfection.* That's what life will be for those who belong to Christ. We will be granted the crown of life, awarded the perfect, complete life—one which is not and cannot be now, but will come *then.*

Those of us who know the Almighty Creator, the only Rescuer of the world, also believe such a life is possible. And we look forward to our lives *then.*

MORE: 2 Timothy 4:7, 8; Revelation 2:10; Revelation 3:10, 11

 RENEWED CREATION

Look! I am creating new heavens and a new earth, and no one will even think about the old ones anymore. Be glad; rejoice forever in my creation!
- ISAIAH 65:17, 18 -

To my mind, the best time to walk is early morning, just as a new day is born, before the world—and my mind and soul—are cluttered with the day's traffic and smudged and torn. I like to be early enough to catch those few seconds when the world seems to hold its breath, wondering at the new day. Then all seems fresh, new, unspoiled, and almost perfect, and there is so much glory that no camera or brush can convey it.

It's an illusion, of course. This world—and my mind and soul—are quite smudged and torn. Any picture we have of "perfection" in this world is far from accurate.

Our souls know that. I believe our souls also feel the connection with nature that, Scripture says, groans under the curse put on it because of man's rebellion against God. All of God's creation is waiting and looking forward to something—yes, something perfect.

I don't understand the breadth of that word *curse,* but I see the results in everything. Poison creeps through the world. Horrible evils claw into our lives and break our hearts. And even in those things in which we take the most joy and satisfaction, we are still aware of imperfection and incompleteness.

Actually, God's creation is in more serious condition than mere smudges and tears. Romans 8 names the real condition: death and decay.

Nothing in this world escapes death and decay.

We know it. We feel it. And we long for cleansing and healing and wholeness. I wonder if this is a longing planted in us by the Spirit when we're given a new life in spiritual realms—a longing that gives us a bit of homesickness and makes us look forward to God's new heaven and earth.

In answer to our longing, God's Word gives us assurance: It's coming! We'll see an entirely new creation, bursting with the freedom of perfection, free of every hint of death and decay.

Many Scriptures promise this new creation. Some of them are old, old prophecies that came even before Jesus' time on earth. I'm sure those prophets, as they passed God's message on to His people, really did wonder how God was going to accomplish all of this. We wonder, too, but I believe we've seen some things those prophets had only an inkling of—the power of resurrection, for one thing, and the establishment of God's new covenant, for another.

The renewed earth will be healed, perfect, complete. One Scripture that speaks great comfort and expectation to me is found in a conversation Jesus had with His disciples. The subject wasn't even about the new creation; instead, they asked, "Just wondering, Jesus, what reward will there be for us in your kingdom? We've left everything of our old life behind to join up with you, and we're wondering... um... what will we get in return?"

Yes, they actually voiced that question to Jesus.

And in His response, I find this exciting remark: "When the world is made new and the Son of Man sits upon his glorious throne..." (Matthew 19:28).

That's not the main point of His answer, but

He said this just as casually as I say, "When I go to Dover tomorrow..."

He said it because it will happen. God has assured us that whatever He plans will come to pass. And He's planning that just as our old bodies will be gone and we will have new ones, so too will heaven and earth be recreated. (Did it occur to you that Scripture says even *heaven* will be new?)

"And no one will even think about the old ones anymore." Isaiah didn't put an exclamation mark after that, but he should have. Our opening verse goes on, with God saying: "Enjoy it forever!" He originally made this magnificent world to be enjoyed; the grandeur of the new world coming is beyond my imagination, but we will enjoy it forever.

This is a hope we hold on to: When Christ sits on His throne, His people will be living on a new earth. A gloriously new earth, joined with heaven, free from all effects of the curse it is now under. We'll get to enjoy His new creation.

The last book of the Bible hearkens back to the opening chapters of Genesis, describing the new world by looking back at God's first perfect Eden. When God created and put mankind in the garden, that place was referred to as *paradise.* Then Adam and Eve chose to go their own way instead of God's way, and they were barred from paradise. We read the word only two places in the New Testament until we get to Revelation 2:7, and there it is almost startling to see the word again. Revelation 2:7 says that one of the rewards Christ promises is "fruit from the tree of life in the paradise of God."

One man's sin lost paradise for all of us until another man's sacrifice made paradise possible once again. The new world, free of decay and death, will be a world restored to the beauty, majesty, and freedom the Creator intended from the very beginning in Eden.

The old heaven and earth will be rolled up like a scroll, and the new will take its place. This prophecy is most likely metaphoric—"rolling up" what is finished and bringing out the new may be similar to our saying we "wrapped it up." Other prophecies speak of the world being destroyed by fire. We do not know the details of how the old heaven and earth will disappear and the new will appear as God's glorious new creation. Only God knows how it will all happen. But He says He will do it.

I believe Him. I'm looking forward to that world.

Early in the mornings, I sometimes feel the earth pause for a millisecond, poised at the edge of a new day. And at those times, I can feel the expectation as creation wonders, *Will this be the day?*

MORE: *Romans* 8:20-22; *2 Peter* 3:13; *Revelation* 6:14; *Revelation* 21:1, 5

 JUDGMENT

*The godly can look forward to a reward, while the wicked
can expect only judgment.*

- **PROVERBS 11:23** -

We will return to dust. We're destined to die. We all know that, believers and unbelievers alike. In the Word of God, our destiny is set in the opening chapters of Genesis.

Then, between Genesis and Revelation, we see two clear paths emerging. Everyone is faced with the choice of a path in life, either the one that leads to God or the one that ignores and snubs God and purposely opposes Him.

> For the LORD watches over the path of the godly, but the path of the wicked leads to destruction. (Psalm 1:6)

Hebrews 9:27 tells us the rest of the story. Our bodies may return to dust, but *then* comes judgment.

Judgment. Although we use the word in so many contexts, some even with good connotations, that combination of letters and sounds can send darts of fear into our hearts.

Jesus told several stories about a "sorting out" that is coming. One example referred to fishermen who sorted out all the fish in their net, keeping the good fish and throwing the bad ones away. "That is the way it will be at the end of the world. The angels will come and separate the wicked people from the righteous" (Matthew 13:49). Another parable pictured wheat and weeds growing together until the end of the world when "the Son of Man will send his angels, and they will remove from his Kingdom everything that causes sin and all who do evil" (Matthew 13:41).

In both cases, the evil is destroyed. The bad fish and the weeds are thrown into the fiery furnace of God's punishment, where there is great, unending agony.

Judgment will be that "sorting out." Throwing away the bad, keeping the good. Judgment is necessary because God is a God of justice. He holds all power and authority, and although we may not see His justice now, He assures us He does have a day of reckoning coming. He will punish all who are so arrogant that they stand against Him. He hates evil. He will not give it any place in His new world. And so every person will have judgment pronounced one day. And the sorting will be carried out.

The first two Scriptures quoted in this meditation tell us about the ultimate destination of each path. One path is watched over, protected, blessed, and rewarded by the Lord. The other path leads only to judgment and destruction.

The "destruction" described in John's vision in Revelation is a lake of burning fire, a place of constant torment that never ends. It's a terrible thing to try to imagine. Revelation sees that day of God's great wrath, when everyone will try to hide from Him. It's useless, of course. Nothing is hidden from God. Even our deepest secret lives are known to Him and will be judged.

God foresees all the arguments against the eternal punishment we call hell. He knows that many will scoff and debate and downplay and deny. He knows there will be many who say they do not believe or care. He knows there will even be Christ followers who refuse to believe the very words of Christ, warning us so sternly about hell.

Why are we dwelling on this now? Two reasons. One, God assures us of His justice. In His new world, the wicked will be repaid for all they've done, and there will be no place for them with God's people in the new world. And reason two: We have great news about this coming judgment!

> For God chose to save us through our Lord
> Jesus Christ, not to pour out his anger on us.
> Christ died for us so that, whether we are
> dead or alive when he returns, we can live
> with him forever. (1 Thessalonians 5:9, 10)

There's no denying that we've all deserved God's anger. We deserve to be thrown out with the bad. But He still wanted to give us a way to come back to Him. And that's what Jesus became—the Way.

The way to know God, the way to approach God, the way to become a child of God, the way to have eternal life, the way to obtain forgiveness. Jesus is the "stairway to heaven," the one who connected us to all God has to offer His children.

"He is the one who has rescued us from the terrors of the coming judgment" (1 Thessalonians 1:10).

We do not need to entertain any fear when we think about standing before God's judgment throne. God's plan to save us from eternal punishment was carried out by Jesus, a man who was willing to take the punishment for us so that we would not have to be condemned. And this forgiveness for what we've done—it's a gift. A gift given to those who believe.

Chapters 2 and 3 of Revelation give us a look at Jesus Christ's messages to churches. These messages are for churches in all eras, and they address issues of all eras. The message to the church in Sardis holds an image that has captured my hope.

Jesus Christ will be the judge of all. His message to the Sardis church was that those who did not soil their robes with evil and who were victorious would be clothed in white, the clothes of a victor. Their names would never be blotted from the Book of Life and—are you ready?—He will announce that they belong to Him.

My hope can see it: I step up to face the Judge. He doesn't even need to check the lists in the book. He looks at me, with the loving eyes of my forever Shepherd, and He says, "This is Elaine. She belongs to me."

Put yourself there, my friend.

MORE: John 3:18; John 12:48; Romans 8:1; Romans 10:13; 2 Thessalonians 1:7-9; Revelation 20:12

REWARDS

And it is impossible to please God without faith. Anyone who wants to come to him must believe that God exists and that he rewards those who sincerely seek him.

- **HEBREWS 11:6** -

For each of the chapters in this book, I've kept a file of thoughts and lists of Scripture that address the subject. The file for this chapter kept growing longer and longer. For this one subject alone, on promised rewards, I had twenty-eight pages within the larger file. Now, I need to condense those twenty-eight pages into one short meditation. Twenty-eight full pages of promises of rewards! Where do I start?

Perhaps we'll start with believing that God does reward us for what we do. If we don't believe that, our view of our lives in the "time of perfection" will be too narrow, because God does have a great deal to say about rewards—both now and in the age to come.

Does it sound too immature as a Christian to say we have hope of a reward for what we do? We might think that whatever good we do should be inspired by a "purer" faith—for example, shouldn't we be acting in a certain way simply out of our love for our Rescuer? Or shouldn't our actions spring from our gratitude to Him for all He has done for us? Shouldn't we be exhibiting certain characteristics only because of our passionate desire to behave as God's children?

Those motivations are all good. But let's face it— rewards motivate us.

God knows this, of course. He knows us so well.

I believe God also bestows rewards out of the goodness of His love for us. If I witness an act of kindness by one of my grandchildren, the first impulse of my grandma heart is to reward them in some way—it may be nothing more than a "good for you" or a quick hug, but it is a reward, nevertheless. I do believe God's heart for us is even bigger than a grandma's. He wants to shower His children with goodness.

A file of twenty-eight pages tells you that the Scriptures hold hundreds of references to rewards. And I know I have not collected them all. Maybe the number is in the thousands. Hebrews 11:6 (the opening verse) did surprise me, though. Here we find belief in rewards linked closely to coming to God, faith, and pleasing Him.

Some of these rewards will quickly follow our obedience here on earth. Some of them will come later, "reserved in heaven" for us.

Don't make the mistake of thinking that forgiveness of your sins, escape from hell, and eternal life are part of your rewards. They are not. God has told us plainly that no one can ever earn or achieve that on their own. That's way beyond the "reward" scale. The gift of life in God's new heaven and earth where rewards will be enjoyed is just that—a gift of God's kindness. Accepting the gift that came through Jesus is the only way to have that life. The rewards, then, are further blessings for those who are God's children.

What are the rewards? We don't know. In Revelation, promises to the victorious are couched in figurative language, like *the fruit of the tree of life,* or *being made pillars in the house of God,* or even *they will sit with me upon my throne.* But Scriptures do speak of treasures in heaven that are inexhaustible, riches that no one can steal or destroy. And Jesus said that anyone who must give up home, family, or possessions because they follow Him will receive "a hundred times as much" in return (Matthew 19:29). When I read that short account, I feel, again, that Jesus *knows.* He knows what's waiting for us because He's already seen it.

You'll find the promises everywhere in God's

Word. He wants us to know there will be rewards! Again, I've listed more than usual in the MORE section. This will give you a start. Find your own favorites and savor the hope.

MORE: Matthew 5:11, 12; Matthew 6:3, 4, 6, 17, 18; Matthew 10:42; Luke 6:35; Galatians 6:7, 9, 10; Colossians 3:23-25; 2 Timothy 4:7, 8; Hebrews 10:35, 36; 2 Peter 1:11

STAY UNATTACHED

Those who weep or who rejoice or who buy things should not be absorbed by their weeping or their joy or their possessions. Those who use the things of the world should not become attached to them. For this world as we know it will soon pass away.

– 1 CORINTHIANS 7:30, 31 –

The words above come after a lengthy discourse on marriage and singleness. The apostle Paul wrote that even this important aspect of life—marriage and family—should not absorb us and restrict our sights to an earthly level.

Think about that word *absorbed:* swallowed up, wrapped up, taken in, consumed.

Of course, Paul is not saying that taking care of your family is unimportant. But he is saying that nothing in this world should have such a strong grip on you that it blocks your view of where you're headed. No, not even family.

What is it in my life that swallows me up or consumes me? What has such a hold on my days and my energies that it blocks my view of the new world coming?

Whether there is great grief in your life or wonderful joys or many possessions or exciting pursuits, do not hold on to any of these things too tightly, and do not let them hold you. Because it will all soon be gone.

I think of Moses, who went right on moving ahead with God's plan in spite of what was happening around him, because he kept his eyes on the one who is eternal and on what the Eternal One was doing. Moses and God had quite an adventure together. (Moses was married and had a family, too.)

I think of Paul's accounts of how much he had suffered in his missionary life, and yet he said it was all nothing—it was "light and momentary"— compared to what's ahead and waiting for us.

I think of Jesus, who submitted to the agony and humiliation of ridicule, ostracism, beatings, and a shameful death because of the joy of what He knew His mission would accomplish for all of us in the eternal realm. (He must really love us.)

I think about the rich young man who wanted so very much to be assured that he could have eternal life, yet he turned away, saddened—because there was something he could not let go.

And I think about us, sisters and brothers, running our races, but sometimes weighed down because we insist on holding so tightly to things that will soon be gone, passed away, over and done with.

I ask myself: What am I holding too tightly today? Or what is it that is holding me?

If it's of this earth, it will soon be gone. There's so much more waiting for me.

MORE: Matthew 6:19-21; Hebrews 10:32-36; Hebrews 13:14; 1 Peter 1:4

PRAYER OF PEACE:

But I am trusting you, O LORD, saying, "You are my God!" My future is in your hands.

– **PSALM 31:14, 15** –

THE TIME OF
PERFECTION

⋙ HE'S NEVER SHAKEN ⋘

The LORD's plans stand firm forever; his intentions can
never be shaken. What joy for the nation whose God is the
LORD, whose people he has chosen as his inheritance.

– PSALM 33:11, 12 –

Let's go back to one of our original questions:
Where is the joy?

I hope, in our journey together, you have
found joy in the promises God makes to you. Here
is one more place where we take great joy—that
since we are now children of God, brought into
His household to flourish as His heirs, we will

someday enjoy the victory of His plans.

Because this is what our hope knows: God's plans will win out.

Even now, although the world seems to be filled with so much that would puncture our hope, we know that God's plans are still in place. He says He is the same God who molded dust to make us. He has not changed throughout all of human history. His plans have not changed. They are firmly in place, in progress, and they will all be completed.

> Then the LORD said to me, "Look, Jeremiah! What do you see?" And I replied, "I see a branch from an almond tree." And the LORD said, "That's right, and it means that I am watching, and I will certainly carry out all my plans." (Jeremiah 1:11, 12)

The apostle Paul had a phrase for the accomplishment of all God's plans; he called it "the time of perfection" (1 Corinthians 13:10). The New International Version translates that as "completeness."

When will this time come? Many have studied prophecy and tried to set up timelines, but even the most devoted scholars disagree. Of course! The timing is not for us to know. Jesus said that even He did not know when everything would come about. His instruction to us was to be ready.

Be ready. Stand firm, stay strong, and continue the mission.

Because this is one thing we do know: God's plans will not be shaken. He will do what He said He will do.

We are journeying through this world, strangers here, but headed home. We know God is in charge of both the history of this world and our own journeys. That's why we can let go of our worry and fear and pray the Psalm prayer for this chapter, knowing our future is safe in the hands of the First and the Last.

MORE: Psalm 40:5; Daniel 4:35; Isaiah 25:9; Isaiah 46:10

OUR KING WILL RETURN

Suddenly two white-robed men were standing with the disciples as they watched Jesus disappear into the heavens. "Why are you standing here staring into heaven?" they asked. "Jesus has been taken away from you into heaven, but someday he will return from heaven in the same way you saw him go!"

– ACTS 1:10, 11 AP –

Perhaps the fascination I have with clouds and sky and the light of the heavens was birthed by what I have been taught since I was a little girl. Now I am an adult and, like you, must choose whether to believe the hope... or not. It might be that this point is the strongest test of our belief in what God has said to us.

This is the hope—the certainty—that Jesus is coming back to this earth. If we hold this hope, it changes how we view all of life and death and what is happening in the world around us. It means there is more to come beyond the days we're living now with jobs and bills and sickness and wars and governments and poverty... there is much more to come. And Christ's return will usher in that new age.

Why do we believe this? Do we have evidence it will happen? Does logic point toward this conclusion? Is there any anecdotal experience on which we can base our expectation?

Our hope rests on one thing: God says it will happen.

You remember we were amazed that when Jesus told His disciples He would meet them in Galilee *after* He was raised from the dead, they did not seem to understand. None of them, in that moment, realized what He was telling them. But as they watched Jesus disappear from their sight, I'm sure they heard the words of the angels. For the remainder of the New Testament, in the accounts of the apostles' travels and in their letters, we hear their excitement and eagerness as they talk of Jesus returning to the earth.

Their hope *knew* it would happen.

As the years go by, I grow increasingly dissatisfied with the way we celebrate Christmas. Of course we should observe those "glad tidings of great joy," that a Rescuer arrived to save us. But the great deceiver, the enemy of our souls, has infiltrated our celebrations—and we have allowed him to do so. So why not take back the territory the enemy has taken from us and reshape our Christmas observances? Let's make it not only a remembrance of the baby but an eager anticipation of the coming of our king. Let's spend the greater part of our time celebrating the joy of the future coming—because that day will overshadow everything that has gone before.

Jesus' first mission to our world was to save us from all that was separating us from God. That mission was accomplished through terrible sacrifice as a human like us. He had to be one of us to pay the price for humanity. His next appearance on earth will be as the glorious, victorious king. Throughout Revelation, especially, we hear Him say repeatedly, "I am coming soon!"

What will happen then? Without putting these into a timeline, here are some of the things He says He will do:

- Judge and repay everyone for what they've done (Revelation 22:12)

- Bring to completion our rescue from everything of this world (Hebrews 9:28)

- Destroy all powers opposing God (1 Corinthians 15:24-26)

- Bring heaven and earth together as one kingdom under His rule (Ephesians 1:9, 10)

- Gather His people to be with Him (John 14:3)

- Establish a kingdom of harmony and peace (Isaiah 9:7)

The last item is from a longer passage foreseeing the birth of the child in Bethlehem. The first part of Isaiah 9 describes the kingdom that child would eventually bring into existence, and verse 7 ends with this: "The passionate commitment of the LORD of Heaven's Armies will make this happen!"

The passionate commitment of the Creator God to His creation and His people still holds. His plans are firm. And so this is the hope of all the children of God and citizens of heaven: The Jesus we follow is alive, and He is coming back to this earth.

MORE: Philippians 3:20; Hebrews 9:28; Revelation 22:20

 OUR KING WILL RULE FOREVER

The world has now become the Kingdom of our Lord and of his Christ, and he will reign forever and ever.

- REVELATION 11:15 -

We sat at a table surrounded by stacks of boxes, shelves of books, and cartons of gifts. The Christian bookstore had graciously created a space in its warehouse for this meeting of a group of writers.

I admit to being bored, and my eyes roamed around the big room, taking inventory. High up on a shelf, one box advertised its contents with a large picture attached to the side: a picture of Santa Claus.

There was no backdrop, no setting, nothing in the picture except the bearded, red-clad figure bent in worship with hands clasped in prayer. The artist had captured a spirit of reverence, a soul kneeling before the King of kings. The epitome of the world's Christmas was bowing down to the God of all creation.

No matter what the world thinks of God, He alone rules! Many have turned Christmas into a mere "holiday," but someday every knee will bow to the Baby born in a stable.

I'm writing this during December. These days, Santas dance in windows and perch on housetops and wave from snow-covered yards. But the Spirit reminds me of that kneeling Santa and the Scripture's promise: Every knee will bow, every tongue will confess: "There is only one God, and He is King!"

Prophets of Old Testament times saw this. Daniel saw someone coming "with the clouds of heaven," who was given sovereignty over all races and nations. And not only would He be sole ruler, but "His rule is eternal—it will never end. His kingdom will never be destroyed" (Daniel 7:14).

We have difficulty grasping *eternity* and *eternal*. Our earthly lives are made up of beginnings and endings and the measurement of the time between. Yet Scripture says the eternal has already been planted in us.

Trying to gain a firmer grasp of *eternal*, I went to my concordance and looked up the word. And it did indeed give me a bigger picture. Here's what my concordance reminds me of: (Don't just skim over this list. Savor the eternity in it all.)

- God's eternal covenant with His people
- Eternal life... and an eternal fire of punishment
- His eternal rule and kingdom
- Sin with eternal consequences
- God, worthy of eternal praise
- God's eternal power
- God's eternal plan
- Eternal salvation, eternal rescue

- An eternal inheritance

- Eternal glory

Without even reading the Scriptures listed in the concordance, we have a glimpse—just a tiny taste—of a kingdom *eternal*. A life beyond our time, under a sovereign God with an eternal plan.

As the children of God, we are part of this kingdom that will go far beyond the years between our day of birth and day of death. All people will eventually bow in allegiance to our King, and He alone will rule forever.

MORE: Psalm 22:27-29; Isaiah 45:23; Zechariah 14:9; 1 Corinthians 15:24-28

PRINCE OF PEACE

And I will make a covenant of peace with them, an everlasting covenant.

- EZEKIEL 37:26 -

It had been quite a night! The long, drowsy shift of watching the sheep and trying to stay awake had been split by the radiance of heavenly glory. First one angel, and then a host of them, had burst through the darkness and into the lives of those shepherds with the news: the Messiah had finally arrived! Peace on earth!

They were so excited that, after finding the baby, they spread out in the village, telling the good news.

I write this as dawn creeps over the hills to the east of my own village. A clear pink and purple sky pushes back dark clouds on the horizon, and light seeps into the valley, growing stronger with every line I type. It's an exciting morning outside. The shepherds must have felt great excitement on that morning, too, as they told everyone of the light finally breaking into their history. All would now be well. The light would push away the darkness. Peace on earth would come.

What happened to those shepherds? Were they in the crowds who came to hear Jesus teach thirty years later? Did any of them become disciples? Or, as the child and his parents disappeared into obscurity for the next three decades and nothing seemed to change in their world, did they wonder if it had all been a hoax? Had they been foolish to believe? Over the years, I'm sure they retold their story often to family and friends, but did they ever question what they had seen and heard? Perhaps they eventually fell silent, talking no more about angels and a baby and peace on earth.

Because, after all, peace did not come to earth. Within two years of that night, soldiers of the ruthless King Herod were going through villages, tearing babies from mothers' arms and killing the children. The oppressive Roman rule never loosened, and seventy years later, Jerusalem was devastated by a Roman army ransacking the city, burning the Temple, and slaughtering thousands of the Jewish people.

What had happened to the promise of peace?

You remember, we asked the same thing at the beginning of our journey together.

Long before the Christ-child slept in the manger, there were prophecies that promised He would be the Prince of Peace and would bring "a river of peace and prosperity" (Isaiah 66:12) to God's people.

What does it mean to have peace? Our first response might be that peace is an absence of conflict. A deeper meaning is that it is a sense of harmony, calmness, and tranquility. We speak of peace in three different spheres: in relationships, in circumstances, and within a person.

The baby born in Bethlehem did come to bring peace. His gift of peace to the world and to us individually is still unfolding.

Jesus brought peace, first of all, into our relationship with the Almighty Creator. He made it possible for enemies of God to become children and heirs of God. That peace is a gift, offered to anyone who believes. We can have that peace now.

Jesus also gives a gift of inner peace to His disciples. His peace can guard our hearts and minds and keep us stable and balanced through whatever storms and battles we face. This peace is a miraculous, supernatural peace that comes only from His Spirit working in us. It takes root in our trust in Him and the promises He's given us.

This peace has begun, but it is not yet perfected—as evidenced by the questions we still have and the way in which our harmony and calmness can so quickly drain away. The devil, working through our old nature, fights everything the Spirit does in our life. It's a battle that will go on until the day of perfection. But we are learning! We are learning to trust the Father, Son, and Spirit, and to lean on the everlasting arms that hold us firmly. Peace within is possible, but we grow into it as we trust more and more. Do not give in to despair! He is always working in us. Ask Him for more peace, and then go marching down that path to peace, *praying* about everything, *telling* Him what you need, and *thanking* Him for all He has done and will do.

Peace in the world, though, is one thing that will not come until the time of Jesus' rule. Nations have never been able to exist without discord and conflict between each other and divisions within themselves. A verse in Isaiah says that only when the Lord comes to judge the earth will people learn what is right.

The same can be said about peace. Only when Jesus reigns will we learn to have true peace among the nations. Then the Lord will settle disputes between nations and teach them how to live in peace. Isaiah foresaw the day when war is no more, when weapons disappear or are turned into other useful tools, and the boots of warriors and the blood-stained uniforms are all burned. We'll be done with war.

Peace in every form will come because the Prince of Peace will be in charge and His rule will never end.

MORE: Isaiah 9:6, 7; Micah 4:1-4; Zechariah 9:10

JUSTICE WILL TRIUMPH

But we are looking forward to the new heavens and new earth he has promised, a world filled with God's righteousness.
- 2 PETER 3:13 -

In the world we know today, where widespread evil flourishes, this hope of 2 Peter 3:13 promises a world that seems impossible—but, oh! How we long for this!

Look at your news feed, or pick up any newspaper. Do you have times when you wish you could find some nice, quiet corner of the world that didn't have all this trouble, and you could pack up and spend the rest of your life there? Or perhaps you're just the opposite—you are an activist, someone who believes that only if people get involved will the world ever change. Even if you are passionate about your cause, does it seem this world is getting better? The news of what is happening today does not bode well for the future, does it?

These conditions are not unique to our time. We hear the voices crying out from Genesis to Revelation: *How long are you going to let the evil go on, Lord? Come right now! Take vengeance on your enemies!*

And above the voices in the world, we hear God's voice saying, "I detest lying and cheating and violence and arrogance. I have a day of reckoning planned." When we read God's words against injustice, we hear His passion for setting things right in His creation, filling the world with rightness, and banishing the evil and wrongdoing.

That is His promise for the time of perfection. Christ the King will bring justice to the entire world. Isaiah 42 looks forward to the time of Christ's reign, and establishing justice is one of the first things mentioned. "He will bring justice to all who have been wronged. He will not falter or lose heart until justice prevails throughout the earth. Even distant lands beyond the sea will wait for his instructions" (Isaiah 42:3, 4).

He will deliver justice. He has an appointed day for judgment, even though many claim they don't believe in God's final judgment or even that God exists at all. But God's promise is that the day will come when He avenges all evil and banishes it from His new heaven and earth. Yes, even the source of all evil, the devil, will be thrown out and punished forever.

Not only will Christ the King deliver vengeance, but He will also instruct and lead the world in bringing justice to all so that His pure justice becomes established and is the guiding rule. Isaiah 2 describes the vision of people streaming to God to learn how to live in peace and justice.

It's interesting that in God's description of the future, even nature will celebrate the establishment of justice. Passages describe the sea shouting praises, the rivers clapping their hands, and the hills singing out with joy when God finally comes to bring His justice and to create a world where evil has no place.

An amazing hope we have! Unbelievable, some might say. But, as we've declared before, our hope is in the Almighty God of impossibles. And this is one of His promises to His children: They will live in a world of purity, justice, and goodness.

We have a long way to go until we see that day, don't we? Or maybe not. Only God knows when all of these things will come to pass. Our hope does know, though, that God's plan will be accomplished. And in the time of perfection, all those headlines of today will be forgotten and it will be true of our world when we say, "as the waters fill the seas, so the earth [is] filled with people who know the LORD" (Isaiah 11:9).

Savor this hope. What a day that will be—what a world that will be!

MORE: Psalm 37:9-20; Isaiah 26:9; Isaiah 51:4, 5; Matthew 12:20; Acts 17:31; 2 Peter 2:9; Revelation 20:10, 14

RENEWAL FREEDOM

But for you who fear my name, the sun of Righteousness will rise with healing in his wings. And you will go free, leaping with joy like calves let out to pasture.
- MALACHI 4:2 -

The opening verse may not mean anything to you. But if you've been raised on a farm, you may have a vivid picture in your mind. I always enjoyed that scene in the spring, when cattle that had been cooped up in our barn for long winter days were first let out to pasture. It wasn't only the young calves that kicked up their heels in the joy of freedom. Even stately old matrons—the cows— would frolic in the fresh air and sunshine with heads tossing, tails flying, and hooves kicking up fresh pieces of soft sod.

I see that joy every time I read Malachi 4:2. It's a picture of the joy we will feel in the freedom of the new heaven and earth. Everything in creation will be free of all that has cursed, plagued, and pained us.

In the history of God's interaction with His people and the world in general, you can't miss that God is a God who makes all things new. Look at all the words in Scripture that point to this work of God. He redeems. He restores. He renews. Re-creates. Cleanses. Purifies. Washes. Redeems. Regenerates. Reconciles. Resurrects.

Those words all speak of reclaiming what was lost, of making all things *new*.

He created His beautiful world. He put mankind here to tend the creation. Humans decided, however, they'd rather go their own way.

Did He wipe us out? No. Did He turn His back and say we were a lost cause? No.

Instead, He makes things new. Renewing. He's been promising it and doing it since Genesis. He's turned wildernesses into gardens and deserts into oases. He brings dry bones to life. He gave us new life and keeps on creating us anew. At this very moment, I'm sure there are some of His children confessing sin... and He will cleanse them. He'll continue renewing, redeeming, cleansing, and purifying until, at the end of this earth's life, the One on the throne will make everything new—not only His people but also this world and even heaven!

> And the one sitting on the throne said,
> "Look, I am making everything new!" And
> then he said to me, "Write this down, for
> what I tell you is trustworthy and true." And
> he also said, "It is finished! I am the Alpha
> and the Omega—the Beginning and the End."
> (Revelation 21:5, 6)

The Almighty Creator is the beginning and end of our history. In the time of perfection, His renewal of His creation will come in many ways. We're given various images that represent the healing:

The river of healing. Both Ezekiel and John saw visions of a river that flows from the presence of God (from His temple, in Ezekiel, and from His throne, in Revelation). Everywhere its waters flow, life will flourish. Even in the Dead Sea, which is now so salty that the usual fish and plants cannot survive there, life will be abundant.

The tree of life. You remember that the tree of life was first in the Garden of Eden. Then Adam and Eve were cut off from eating of that fruit and thus were destined to die. Now, God's people will not only eat the fruit of that tree, but its leaves will be used for healing and restorative purposes.

No more curse. All of creation is under the curse of decay and death, but there will be no more of that in God's new heaven and earth! All that brought tears and sorrow and pain will be gone.

Restored relationship. Revelation 22:3, 4 tells us that the throne of God and the Lamb will be in the city, in the midst of God's people. They will worship Him, and "see His face!" And the Great Shepherd will continue to care for His flock, leading them to "springs of living water" (Revelation 7:17). Forever.

In the beginning, God created and said it was very good. Now we're waiting for the day when God's new creation comes to the time of restoration and perfection, and it will be very good once more.

The curse of sin through disobedience brought into our world everything from bugs that nibble on our gardens to cancer that eats our bodies and hatred that consumes hearts and minds. Whatever results of the curse you are struggling with today, your hope can know that God plans to remove that from your life and restore to you the life intended for God's children. In the day of perfection, your world and your life will be healed. There is great joy ahead!

MORE: Romans 8:21; 1 Peter 1:6; Revelation 22:1-5

POSSESSED FOR PERFECTION

We, too, wait with eager hope for the day when God will give us our full rights as his adopted children.

- **ROMANS 8:23** -

The story of the prodigal son often moves me to tears. I can visualize the father, who has waited so long, watching, hoping, and finally welcoming his son home. Then, contrary to all expectations, logic, and tradition, he reinstates the prodigal into the family!

All of us who are now children of God know what it is to be the prodigal, undeserving, but forgiven and welcomed back. We'll celebrate that forgiveness for all of our earthly lives.

But at the "time of perfection" for each of us, the day when God welcomes His sons and daughters home—that day will be even grander! The father of the prodigal threw a party to celebrate his son's return. 2 Peter 1:11 (BSB) talks of a "lavish reception" into Christ's kingdom for heirs of the Father. Other translations use the words *grand reception, rich welcome,* and *glorious entrance.*

And then we'll be granted our full rights as God's children.

We've already pondered the amazing hope that we will have new bodies and there will be rewards. But there is apparently so much more! For one thing, this transformation that God has already begun in us will be brought to completion. John wrote:

> Dear friends, we are already God's children, but he has not yet shown us what we will be like when Christ appears. But we do know that we will be like him, for we will see him as he really is. And all who have this eager expectation will keep themselves pure, just as he is pure. (1 John 3:2, 3)

We don't know what we will be, but God has told us enough that our hope is eager to see that day.

We know that the Spirit has already been at work in us, changing us to be like Jesus. Paul wrote a letter as he approached the end of his life, describing his determination to forget whatever was behind and look forward to what was ahead, always pressing on "to possess that perfection for which Christ Jesus first possessed me" (Philippians 3:12). He was not perfect and he acknowledged it (and he had quite a "past," too!), but he was looking forward to being perfect.

Was Paul a "special" person, that Christ Jesus chose him to be perfect? No.

Perfection was the plan for you from the moment you became a believer—actually, even *before* you believed. God's plan from the beginning was that *all* of His children would be brought to completeness, fully like their brother, Jesus.

Oh, read that last sentence again! What an audacious thing for us to claim! But God said it first. And He says our hope can be certain of this.

Remember that in the beginning, God created humans to be like Him. I think we often miss the power of that because we have lived so long with these dying bodies and sinful natures—so *unlike* Him—that we lose the significance of what we were meant to be in the first place. God intends to restore what we lost.

Go back to the passage from 1 John: What does it mean to be like Jesus? I don't know. I can't imagine. We can only look forward to it and say, "Wow! What will that be like?"

John was one of the three disciples on the mountain with Jesus when the curtain of eternity opened and the disciples saw Jesus in all His glory, talking with Moses and Elijah. The three disciples saw something of eternity and people living in eternity. Later, John also witnessed Jesus on this earth with a new, resurrected body. Surely those experiences inspired John's hope as he wrote about what we will be in the day of completion.

I do not yet understand how seeing Jesus "as He is" will complete the transformation, but I suspect that knowing Christ fully, being with Him face to face, will have a transformative effect on us all. We know that even now, the more time we spend with our Lord, the more He can change our minds, hearts, thoughts, and actions. Yet our sight is clouded. When we see Him clearly and when we are fully *with* Him, what exciting and incredible things will surely happen to all of us who love Him?

I take from this another promise: I will someday see His love clearly. I'll be able to see it on His face and in His eyes and feel it in His touch and hear it in His voice, and I will finally understand the love that is so deep and wide and beyond my comprehension now. We know that in our life here, being loved has transforming powers. Perhaps knowing Christ's love fully and finally seeing its depth will transform us completely. For now, it is enough for me to know that I will see Him and know, face to face, how much He loves me.

So, John writes, let's work at keeping ourselves pure because we are headed for this exciting future. We work at it, but of course John knew, just as we know today, that perfection in this world is impossible—we still stumble and fall short of Christ's purity and sinlessness. John knew this reality, and he reminds us (1 John 1:9) that God uses even our sin and confession to cleanse and change us, working toward the future promise of our complete transformation.

I've gotten caught up in thinking about our completeness and perfection. But there are other "rights" of the children of God. What will they be? We don't know that yet, but in His Word to us, God promises repeatedly that a priceless inheritance is waiting for us. We'll see it all someday.

MORE: Philippians 1:6; Hebrews 2:9, 10; 1 Peter 1:4; Revelation 21:7

 **HOME**

With your unfailing love you lead the people you have redeemed. In your might, you guide them to your sacred home.

- EXODUS 15:13 -

If we begin to read the account of God's relationship to His people, we aren't very far into the Scriptures before we see what His goal is: He wants to bring them home to Him. The opening verse is from a song of Moses, composed after the rescue at the Red Sea. Moses saw it, way back then. He knew God had long-range plans to guide His people through their earthly journeys to come home to Him in His eternal kingdom.

Throughout Scripture, we see all God has done to restore our relationship with Him. He brought the Israelites out of Egypt to be His people. In the wilderness, He came to dwell with them in the Tabernacle, giving them visual evidence of His presence with them. Through the prophets, He said,

"I want you to know me—more than I want religious rituals." The Messiah who was foretold was called "Immanuel," God with us. We hear Jesus praying in Gethsemane, telling His Father that He wanted His disciples to be with Him where He was going.

We know that this reconciliation of relationship was the reason Jesus came: "Christ suffered for our sins once for all time. He never sinned, but he died for sinners to bring you safely home to God" (1 Peter 3:18). 1 Thessalonians tells us about the pivotal point: God chose to save us and not pour out His anger on us.

After Jesus left the earth, the Holy Spirit came to dwell with God's children. Before He left, Jesus promised that He and His Father would come to each obedient disciple and "we will come and make our home with each of them" (John 14:23). God is already living with His children, although not in the sense that we can physically detect Him. Yet it's a very personal relationship—He says our bodies are His temple and His dwelling place. That's beyond our comprehension, but it tells us how closely He lives with us, and how intimately He wants to be involved in our lives.

And so, in the grand finale of perfection, God will bring together the new heaven and the new earth and make His home in the midst of His people. It will be the heavenly city built by God for His people, the place they immediately know as their homeland. His Temple and His throne will be in the new Jerusalem, the holy city.

There, in that new world, God will be home with His people, and His children will finally be home with Him, where He will always provide, care for, and guide His children. We find the description of that life in Revelation 21:4, that appealing declaration that there will be no more pain, death, sorrow, or crying.

In John 14:3, Jesus has a word of assurance for every one of His disciples, you and me included: "When everything is ready, I will come and get you, so that you will always be with me where I am."

Don't you wonder what it is that He has to prepare? Whatever it is, I believe each one of us will find it is "home." It will be made to suit us perfectly. Because there we will finally be living the life we were meant to live all along, a life together with our Great Shepherd and Almighty King.

MORE: *1 Thessalonians 5:9, 10; Ezekiel 37:27-28; Revelation 21:3, 4; Jude 1:24*

Surely your goodness and unfailing love will

pursue me all the days of my life, and I will live

in the house of the LORD forever.

- **PSALM 23:6** -

MANY THANKS

This Hope Knows journey has stretched over fifteen years. Many people have helped me along the way, and although I've already expressed my thanks to most of you privately, it's time to publish my gratitude.

The team at JPV Press has been terrific. They handled this project with great care, and their enthusiasm and patience carried me through. The one thing I appreciate most about them is their commitment to "an audience of one." Without that mutual guiding star, our teamwork would never have happened.

This last book, especially, has come through many fierce battles. Thanks to my staunch warriors in prayer, Cheryl, Mary Jane, and Meadow. I know prayers also came from the Maine Ladies and my turtle shell—I may not know who prayed, but I knew the battle had changed and your prayers made a difference. Rosie, you know that your constant question of, "When is that book going to be finished?" was one of the primary reasons the first book in the Hope Knows series ever saw publication. Oh, and Emily, thanks for that one day in particular when I just needed a few chuckles, and you provided them! (You probably don't even remember it, but it changed my day.)

Thanks to Noel, the Maine Ladies, and Paul. You have all added to my life and work in so many various and important ways that a few words here could never describe the scope of your influence.

My greatest thanks to my heavenly Father, my Rescuer Jesus, and my Guide and Comforter, the Spirit. Only God could have given me this life. He gets all the credit.

BOOK ONE

Followers of Jesus may believe in a perfect life coming someday in the future, but what about today? How do I get through today? This book shares reflections on what hope knows about today.

BOOK TWO

This book isn't about the messes in our lives. It's about the hope for our past that breaks those chains and opens those prison doors. *Is there any hope for what's happened in my past?* God says, "Yes!"

FOR MORE INFORMATION, VISIT WWW.JPVPRESS.COM

BOOK THREE

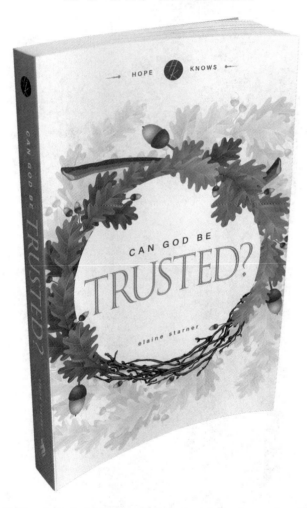

Fellow pilgrim, this book does not intend to wheedle, manipulate, or coax you to hope and trust in my Heavenly Father. It's only purpose is to share with you the One who has given me new life.

BOOK FOUR

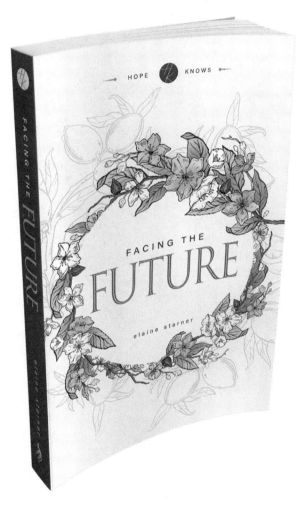

What is coming tomorrow? As we stand on the threshold of the next hour, the next day, the next year, how can we go on with courage, peace, and even joy? We may not be able to see what the road ahead is like, but there are certainties about the future our hope can know.

FOR MORE INFORMATION, VISIT WWW.JPVPRESS.COM